What Nobody Tells You About Getting Older

Aging with Both Eyes Open and a Smile on Your Lips

Mary Westheimer

Illustrations by Robert Chambers

Penstemon Press

Penstemon Press

penstemonpress.com
info@penstemonpress.com

Paperback edition ISBN 979-89991565-0-1
Hardcover edition ISBN 979-89991565-1-8
ePub edition 979-89991565-2-5

BISAC:

SEL005000 - SELF-HELP / Aging
HEA010000 - HEALTH & FITNESS / Healthy Living

Contents

Introduction...7

SEEING, FEELING, ACTING

Saving Beyond Value 14
Less Patience for Foolishness 16
Sing, Sing, Sing 18
"I Just Don't Understand".................................. 20
Younger Friends 22
You Must Remember This (or Not) 23
The Party's Over 26
Loss Leaders.. 28

OH, MY BODY!

Skin in the Game 34
Rough Edges.. 36
Earlobes and Arm Flaps 38
Attack of the Pollock Spots 40
Tattoo Evolution 42
Making Up 44
Suit Up 46
Radical Reinforcements 48
"I'll Be Right Back" 50

Necklines Never in Style. 52
Hair Today. 54
Muscle Misfire. 56
The Knee Bone's Connected to 58
Say Can You See 60
The Eyes Have It 62
Now Hear This. 64
Speak Up 66
Hang On. 67
Wear and Tear (No Warranty) 68
Can't, Not Won't 70
Why All the Buffets in Sun City Are Full at 5 p.m. 72
We Make a Lot More Noises 74
Sex Isn't What It Used to Be 76
Balancing Act. 78

THINK ABOUT THE GOOD THINGS

It's Easier to Recognize the Small Stuff 84
We're More Inclined to Speak Honestly 86
We Get Better at Picking Friends. 88
We Finally Like the Music in the Grocery Store 90
Payback Time. 91
We Shed the 'Shoulds'. 92
We Get Smarter. 94
We're Expected to Celebrate Our Birthday Months. 95
We Finally Like Naps and Baths 96

Less Close Shave.. 98

What Goes Around Comes Around 100

We Pretty Much Do What We Want to Do.......................... 102

Change Is Good... 104

BUT WHAT CAN WE DO?

Dead or Alive 110

Get a Move On... 113

Attitude Is Everything 114

Eat It 116

Believing Is Being... 118

Abandon Expectations.. 120

Put a Sock in It 122

Sex? Yes 124

Nipping and Tucking 126

Stay Curious.. 128

Cool Shoes, Twinkly Tiaras, and Purple Hair 130

Be Silly 132

Really Do Eat Dessert First 134

Acknowledgments.. 136

About the Author.. 138

About the Illustrator 140

Index.. 142

Introduction

Whatever you think about aging is probably wrong.

Even though the things you once thought about old people are now probably about you, you likely had them wrong because no one really tells us what aging is going to be like, possibly because, if we knew, we might kill ourselves.

Or would we be relieved that sagging skin and cluelessness aren't just our personal failings?

It is not out of the question that someone, oh, maybe my mom, tried to tell me some of these things, but it is also a good possibility that I just didn't listen. After all, she was my mom. What could she know? Perhaps if she had said, "Mary! It's the future calling!" I might have listened. But I doubt it.

I thought I knew what it meant to get older—being wiser seemed like a Good Thing—but I didn't really understand it. Life isn't just an accumulation of wisdom as I'd thought, because the ground keeps shifting. Except for fundamental facts, like gravity, things aren't static.

What was true today gets turned on its head tomorrow. So any tips for memorizing when it was cheaper to call long distance—a once time-honored money-saving hack—are totally useless now that we are almost all using mobile phones, and in many situations, the current time and our current location doesn't matter.

Unless they tell me, I often don't know where people are and, because I use autodial, I don't even know the phone numbers of my dearest relatives and friends.

This unfortunate lack of awareness of the realities of aging can lead to curmudgeonism. It takes great strength of character to never say, "I remember when [something, anything] was better before." It may have indeed been better before, like healthier food, but it also might just be that the fairy dust of memory obscures the negatives. (Remember when we were thrilled that a car lasted 80,000 miles? Now we're disappointed if it doesn't last 200,000).

Think about your aunt pinching your cheek and saying, "You look so young!" (This actually happened to me. I was a teenager and knew everything, so it was particularly horrifying.) What I realize now is that, when I see younger people—say a doctor who looks ten years old (whom I affectionately refer to as "Doogies" in honor of *Doogie Howser, M.D.,* the TV show featuring a precocious character who became a doctor at age fourteen), they look so young because *I don't feel as old as I am.* They must be ten because I'm only forty-seven (that's just a shade more than two decades off).

Yes, most of the surprising aspects of aging are a revelation, and sadly most of them suck. A great number are body related. Time will tell if the millennials who practically live at the gym fare better or wear out sooner, but those who have reached "a certain age" are learning our bodies seem to have "best before" dates we weren't privy to.

Some of it, too, is attitude. If I literally bit my tongue every time I thought things were better before, I'd be speechless, which might make some people happier. Instead, I try to focus on the bright side.

And there is a bright side. While there are many unhappy surprises about getting older, thank goodness the positive ones outweigh those negatives.

I share those saving graces as well as things you can do—or not do, since, after all, you are an adult making your own decisions—to stave off the ravages of aging.

Except for entries based on personal stories, everything has been researched and fact-checked.

I hope the following observations are enlightening, guffaw inducing, and perhaps even worth sharing with others who also are heading into the aging abyss.

I might have done things differently if I'd known—worked out when I was younger, not been so hard on my body, skipped a few rock concerts, and so much more—and the rest I want to laugh about.

So let's laugh.

—Mary Westheimer

PART 1

Seeing
Feeling
Acting

The mountain looks different from the top than it does from the bottom. These days I do things that used to make me cringe, but now I usually know why. And I usually don't care what others think of me for doing them.

Some are good, some are bad, and some now finally make sense, although I'm not entirely happy about that . . .

Saving Beyond Value

I'm not a hoarder, but I am a saver. I save all sorts of things, many of which I cannot remember why I saved them. Sometimes I don't even remember what they are. Some I keep for decades, like the boxes of VCR tapes I saved so long they're no good anymore (unless you have a cultural icon museum).

Saving things is fine if I still like them, but if they are just a physical representation of a long-lost memory, it may be time to invoke early Marie Kondo, a master of saving only what you love.

I like to break my purges into chunks—divide and conquer has become one of my favorite strategies—and clean up one room or even a single drawer at a time. It feels surprisingly good, which is why I wonder why I still struggle to do it. Yet after every trip to St. Vincent de Paul I feel lighter, and definitely worthy of some ice cream.

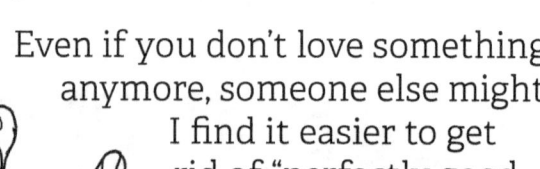

Even if you don't love something anymore, someone else might. I find it easier to get rid of "perfectly good things!" if I know someone else can use them.

There are websites like Buy Nothing (buynothingproject.org), OfferUp (offerup.com), and FreeCycle (freecycle.org) as well as local organizations where you can shed things that you no longer want or need.

Swap 'til You Drop

One fun way to pass along clothing you no longer love (or, er, fit) is a clothing swap. The concept is simple: Everyone brings bags of clean, good-condition clothing and shoes that they no longer wear. The host usually sets up mirrors and a makeshift changing room, items are sorted by type, and the fun begins. The goal is to see your no-longer-cherished items go to folks who love them, and to find a few amazing finds yourself (but fewer than you brought). Whatever isn't taken is donated to a worthy charity. Search for "Clothing Swap" in your area on Facebook, NextDoor, or your favorite search engine. Or if you're up for it, why not host your own? Even a few friends of similar size and fashion sense can have a great time without it being a big to-do. For inspiration, check out hints and upcoming events from the OG queen of clothing swaps, Suzanne Agasi, at clothingswap.com.

Less Patience for Foolishness

After you have "been there, done that" for a while, it becomes exponentially more difficult to accept the ideas and actions of people who are naïve or unwilling to accept reality.

Fortunately, you can usually just step away. A teacher once taught me one wonderful way to do that. The first time a parent came in for a conference and said, "I'm getting divorced," she sympathized. The woman assured her the divorce was a good thing.

The next time a parent came in and announced that she, too, was getting a divorce, the teacher carefully asked, "Is this a good thing or a bad thing?" (It was a bad thing.)

Now educated, the teacher told us, "Now I just say, 'Wow!'"

"Wow!" covers a lot of territory. You don't have to agree with the person, or even comment, you just have to indicate you are listening.

Beware, however, of "Uh-huh." People catch onto that pretty quickly as a sign you may be trying to placate them, or aren't listening at all.

Sing, Sing, Sing

As an older person, you may find yourself singing in unison with your partner or friends when you hear something that reminds you of a particular song.

Just think how many songs you've heard during your life! You have plenty of source material and memories that link to it.

Usually, you can just sing a line or two, though—who can remember all the lyrics or the entire tune? But it's enough to bring back happy memories, which makes it worthwhile, even if people around you cringe.

My maternal grandparents, whom I loved dearly, did this. Then I snickered. Now I sing.

"I Just Don't Understand . . ."

As I age, I understand less and less of what is going on. More and more of my sentences begin, "I just don't understand why . . ."

Famous musical artists and actors are often unknown to me. In ads for shows and concerts. I sometimes don't recognize any of the names at all, yet I'm assured by others that they are indeed legendary and important.

It's clear from their attire, homes, cars, and jewelry that they are also rich, although it befuddles me why since I have no idea what they even do.

That lack of understanding is accelerated by computers, social media, and a tsunami of TV, audio, and payment options. I can make computers pretty much do what I want but thank goodness my needs are limited.

I have never understood why anyone would invest in crypto or NFTs, but so far, I haven't needed to.

I've realized that most of what I don't understand really doesn't matter to me since it has no bearing on my life. That is a relief and the lifting of a great burden. I'm actually navigating pretty well considering I don't understand much of anything.

Younger Friends

Having younger friends provides a helpful counterweight to aging. While I don't always understand their thinking, I like having people I can call on to explain things like why you would pay for pants that are already ripped. (I still don't understand, but I am open to grasping it.)

As you get older, the need for younger people in your life is especially important if you don't have kids—kids and their friends are excellent resources. Younger friends keep me tapped into what is happening even though it still may not make sense to me.

Be sure to cultivate older friends, too. We need them in our lives so that we can feel young. My husband and I used to go out for breakfast with the ROMEOS ("Retired Old Men Eating Out," honoring a group my father dined with), who were in their eighties and nineties.

We loved their stories, as well as their wisdom and irreverence, and they liked that we knew how to search the Internet.

Yes, the contemporary circle of life.

You Must Remember This (Or Not)

One side effect of aging that most of us readily recognize is our loss of memory. Often underlying that recognition is the fear that we are slipping into some form of dementia. Usually, though, we just can't remember anything.

We are not alone. The inability to recall names, places, dates, and people we have known for fifty years is one of the things almost all older people share. A friend recently told me, "I can remember your name or your face but not both. Pick one." I appreciated her offer to let me choose, but honestly, I have little confidence she'll remember which one I preferred, much less who I am.

There is good reason for our memory challenges. Some memories indeed fade as time passes, but most of the time it's the burden of increased information competing with what we already have stored. The information may be there, but we may have trouble retrieving the memory we want.

The more unique and distinctive the event, however—a wedding, a historic event, a first raise—the more likely we'll remember it. Many things don't make it into our long-term memory at all, so retrieval is harder. Linking to other memories ("Sallie, Ruth and Bob's daughter, lived in Chili, New York") helps connect to several points that might jiggle loose a memory.

There are other things you can do, too. If something is important, rehearse it repeatedly. This helps imprint it in your memory. So does, apparently, sleeping after you learn something. (Yet another good reason for a nap.)

Visualizing an item, person, or place not only helps you remember it, it can help you retrieve its name which otherwise might get stuck on the tip of your tongue. So, when you find yourself frustrated because you can't retrieve the word you want when you want it, try to see the item, smell it, or hear it. Using other senses can bring it forth, much in the way a smell, a photo, or a song can bring back long-forgotten memories when you least expect them.

Long-time partners, friends, and family members might joke about stories they've told so many times that they use a label. I might simply call out, "Story 1532!" My husband and I have so many of these that, if I forget the story number (which, honestly, I just make up on the fly), he's known me long enough to remind me. He doesn't need much prompting to repeat the story himself.

Our memories aren't a total lost cause, though. It turns out that your brain needs a "mental gym" as much as your body needs a physical one. Keep your brain and memory supple by learning new things. When you learn something new, your neurons can grow new projections, form new connections, and maybe even create new neurons.

Finally, avoid overloading your memory, which is full from a lifetime of, well, living. A great way of doing this is to write everything down. Our minds are data processors, not memory banks. As David Allen, author of the wonderful book *Getting Things Done,* observed, the only reason to think about something more than once is because you *like* thinking about it.

Fortunately, technology offers easy-to-access "memory banks." Programs like Evernote (evernote.com) let you keep and share records on your phone, laptop and desktop computers so you can capture a thought anywhere and share it anytime. Amazingly, any time I write something down, another thought pops up like a napkin in a restaurant dispenser.

That being said, establishing the habit of writing everything down can be challenging. Make sure you have tools like note savers to help you and, when you find yourself saying, "I need to remember that" all you really need to remember is to write it down.

Old School

Although there are some advantages to using computers, several studies show that writing by hand is actually the best way to learn, especially for young people. A 2024 Frontiers in Psychology brain EEG study found that students who wrote by hand had higher levels of electrical brain activity in interconnected regions that govern movement, vision, sensory processing, and memory. Ten years earlier, a study by Pam A. Mueller and Daniel M. Oppenheimer revealed that taking notes by hand requires more attention and thought to analyze, consolidate, prioritize, and relate information leading to a deeper understanding of the information.

The Party's Over

If you think you used to be able to handle more alcohol than you can now, you're probably right.

Despite what you were able to drink when you were in college (an amount that may have increased exponentially over many years of storytelling: "One night I drank two six-packs of PBR!"), you have good reason to not be able to hold your liquor like you used to. By the time you're in your forties, your body doesn't break down alcohol as efficiently as it did when you were in college.

As we age, the proportion of fat to muscle in our bodies tends to increase even if our weight stays the same. In addition to more fat—as if we need that—alcohol dehydrogenase, or ADH, one of the three main enzymes in our bodies that digest alcohol, may become less efficient as we age.

And then the liver enzymes that help break down the alcohol and help prevent hangovers also decide to semi-retire.

Meanwhile, the proportion of water in our body tissues declines, leaving less liquid to dissolve alcohol, meaning we absorb a higher concentration of the hard stuff. And don't forget those daily meds many of us may be prescribed as we get older, many of which react badly with alcohol.

All of this probably explains why the Centers for Disease Control and Prevention's current Dietary Guidelines for Americans recommend no more than two drinks daily for men and one for women.

So, yes, it really is you.

And it's also most of us aging people; you are not alone.

That being said, maybe you really didn't need that drink after all.

Loss Leaders

I was only able to get through high school math class by memorizing, but even I can do the mortality "word problem". As we get older, so do most of our friends. Eventually we begin to have health issues and yes, die. The older we get the more friends die more frequently. (Maybe we should discuss the "two trains approaching each other at the same rate of speed" word problem. Even though I probably won't get the answer right, it seems like more fun talking about than us leaving the station.)

Death is increasingly part of our lives as we age, an immutable truth that we can only avoid and deny to some extent. Believing in reincarnation or an afterlife offers relief for some people, but we still will miss the laughter and footsteps of our loved ones.

The deepest tragedy is always the death of young people, and sudden loss can be devastating. But when we watch people suffer, whatever their age, acceptance is easier. Suffering allows the living to let their loved ones go more easily.

No one gets out of here alive. How we handle the demise of our friends, relatives, and other people we love is always difficult, but to see their departure as a release from their pain does make it easier.

But wait, there's more! We lose so many things as we age: our abilities, our stamina, our patience. Those losses are no less real, and they also ask for their own awareness and acceptance.

Acceptance appears to be a frequent stop on this journey. It gives us a chance to settle into What Is and maybe even find another route or destination, an opportunity for grace. And it's as close to driving the train as we're going to get.

PART 2

OH,
MY BODY!

Many of the surprises bestowed by aging have to do with **our bodies** betraying us.

What the heck happened?! I used to just live my life and stayed slim and strong. Now I spend a ridiculous amount of time, energy, and money simply *maintaining* my body.

Whether or not it's my fault, it is my, uh, challenge.

When it comes to your body, though, consider this Amazing Fact: With all of the medical experts in the world, *you* are still the world's greatest authority on you. Only you know how you feel.

If you pay attention, that is. Where is that ache? Does something cause it? Or seem to prevent it? This sort of information, when interpreted by people who study our complex bodies, is invaluable.

So, while you don't have to wear the gloves, mask, booties, and scrub cap, you can be a crucial part of your healthcare team.

Rubber scalpel, please . . .

Skin in the Game

Apparently, neglect is not a good approach to lifelong skin care. Aside from bathing and applying lotion, I didn't do much—and I was not prepared for my skin to simply fail in place.

This is a bigger problem for people like me with fair skin and those who live in dry, sunny climes, but we all have noticed—or experienced—how our skin barely protects us anymore.

Indeed, I began wearing as many adhesive bandages at sixty as I did when I was six (easily resisting the Hello Kitty ones. There *is* a bridge too far, at least for me. But I am thinking there could be a line of stylish bandages for the more mature set, perhaps a collection of tie-dye ones in a rainbow of colors.)

This state of affairs may be because we abandoned our skin first, exposing it to sun that breaks down skin's elastin, the fibers that allow it to stretch and regain its shape to remain firm. The elastin fibers can heal, but after a while they lose their ability to repair our skin. (Remember how your mother warned you about getting too much sun? Yes, she was right.)

Even though my body isn't getting any thinner, my skin is. Caused by loss of collagen, the most abundant protein in our bodies, our skin can start thinning as early as in our twenties, but the problem may only become apparent when it becomes transparent and fragile, often in our sixties.

Collagen maintains our skin's structure and forms the connections between our muscles and bones; it diminishes as we age, which means that our skin becomes less elastic and wrinkles form. The natural fat in the deeper layers of our skin retreats with the collagen, leaving space under our skin that allows the skin to droop or sag where it used to be firm.

You can help keep up your collagen by eating lean and clean protein such as beans, lentils, organic tofu, and fish. Keeping your muscles moving helps too, because it pumps blood and lymph fluid, which supply our skin with oxygen and nutrients, carry away waste products, and support the skin's immune cells.

One result of our skin's deterioration is crepey skin, and crepey skin is creepy skin. That papery feeling and the accompanying waves of wrinkles seem to suddenly appear without warning.

Wrinkling can be genetic, but it isn't helped by smoking, frequent exposure to ultraviolet rays, extreme weight changes, and diets that include a lot of processed foods.

Rough Edges

It somehow seems like a cruel joke that, while our skin thins, we get more tough calluses on our hands and feet. Collagen—or the lack of it—is the cause once again.

As our body's collagen declines, we can have even more issues if we neglect caring for our feet and fingers. Our feet have gotten a lot of use and friction, after all, and if we aren't good about keeping them moisturized and removing the calluses with a pumice stone or manicures and pedicures—something that becomes more of a necessity than a luxury as we age—the calluses can crack and make it hard to walk or stand.

If you live near a beach, you can take advantage of Mother Nature's pedicure by walking where the sand serves as the world's natural callus remover.

Otherwise, perhaps it's time for a spa day. As we age it becomes a medical necessity, but that doesn't mean we can't enjoy it.

Earlobes and Arm Flaps

Our skeletons (except our skulls and pelvises, which leaves ample opportunity for suggestive commentary from which I will kindly refrain) stop growing before we reach twenty. Our noses, earlobes, and ear muscles, however, appear to enlarge.

It's an unfortunate illusion caused by connective tissue and cartilage cells dividing and weakening as we age, allowing these body parts to stretch. Meanwhile, the rest of our body begins to shrink, increasing the contrast and decreasing our dignity.

Perhaps even more humiliating for women are arm flaps, which are also sometimes charmingly referred to as "bat wings." These usually appear suddenly, perhaps because we don't spend much time looking at our arms in the mirror when there are so many other alarming developments to divert our attention.

Upper arm flab can be exacerbated by genetics, hormone levels, stress, reduced activity, and age. Lack of skin elasticity and reduced activity also can allow the skin to hang more loosely, perhaps making things look worse than they are.

The good news: these flaps can be addressed by strength training our triceps with enough of a load, volume, and frequency to fill out the skin underneath our arms.

It goes without saying (but of course I will anyway) that this calls for exercise. If you're overweight, losing body fat will help as you build up your tricep muscles. These muscles on the back of your arms aren't used much in daily activities, but strengthening and building them will help "fill" the flaps.

Try exercises including tricep push ups, tricep step-ups, tricep dips—none of which require fancy equipment—to see results in four to six weeks. You may want adult supervision (not to mention accountability) to work on these exercises or use them as a quest to pursue at the gym.

Attack of the Pollock Spots

If skin aberrations weren't enough of a surprise, some of us have found ourselves adorned with splotches and blotches that, in more positive moments, we can allow to transport us to thinking about the transformative paintings of Jackson P.

The deep purple blotches that seem to magically appear on my arms are, it turns out, purpura, which sounds far more romantic than it is. When small blood vessels leak under our thinning skin's surface, purpura appears as red, purple, and brown blood spots.

Purpura can be caused by drug interactions (blood pressure medication is a prime suspect), vitamin deficiencies, or congenital disorders, as well as sun exposure. The slightest touch can result in what looks like the aftermath of a street fight.

I have learned that, following said "slightest touch"—exacerbated by the tendency to lose my balance more easily—I can sometimes stave off the Darkening (which now sounds like a horror movie, and may just be one) by quickly rubbing a broad area around where I just bumped. That allows the blood to disperse before pooling and saves me a blotch or two.

But that's not the end of our new abstract expressionist phase! Age, or liver, spots are smaller, flat brown spots caused by too much sun. They vary in size and usually appear on areas that have been exposed to the sun, such as the face, hands, shoulders, and arms. The blotches can be lightened or removed, but they can then come back like a bad high-school friend.

Perhaps we should just get tattoos to make them into small animals.

Speaking of tattoos . . .

Tattoo Evolution

When the canvas changes, so does the art. That definitely applies to tattoos. As a young adult, a friend of a friend decided to get a discreet, cute Winnie-the-Pooh tattoo on her hip. Unfortunately, after a couple of decades and two kids, Winnie became a grizzly.

Even if you don't end up with a grizzly bear, tattoos often fade as cells from your immune system called macrophages absorb and disperse the ink on your skin. Intricate tattoos can blur as well as stretch as your body wrinkles and loses elasticity.

The most visible changes in large tattoos are in places most prone to stretching, such as the abdomen, upper arms, thighs, side and lower back. Sunlight, smoking, and friction can all accelerate skin aging and tattoo fading, too.

Of course, they won't fade entirely, although you can have them removed, which I understand hurts even more than having them applied, and we aren't even discussing the pain in your pocketbook. Or perhaps we will find ourselves living among smudged blue people who, in nostalgic moments, remind us of the charming cartoons of our youth.

Tat for Tit

Sometimes tattoos can do more than memorialize your mom or a special moment. Some women choose to use decorative tattoos after a mastectomy. Not unlike a beautiful butterfly emerging from a cocoon, breast cancer surgery survivors can choose subjects like a spray of graceful flowers or free-flying birds like those shown on Pinterest (pinterest.com/pin/100134791708605955/). They need to wait until all scars are healed and treatments such as chemotherapy are completed, but that gives them time to think about what they'd like and to talk to tattoo artists who have done similar work before. The site BreastCancerNow (breastcancernow.org/about-breast-cancer/life-after-treatment/your-body-after-breast-cancer-treatment/decorative-tattoos-after-breast-cancer-surgery) **has a helpful overview on the topic.**

Making Up

If you never wore makeup before, aging may make you and other old dogs try new tricks.

Once again, the sun can be the culprit for skin damage, making your skin blotchy. If you haven't been following a faithful facial routine, you might now wish you had been.

With now being now, however, you may have to resort to just covering up the evidence. So much for my youthful glow—I now have a relationship with the consultants at several Sephoras.

And then there are those bags under your eyes. Despite their possibly suggesting that you are not far from the grave, they are simply mild swelling or puffiness. As we age, the tissue around our eyes weakens and allows the fat that helps support our eyes to move into the lower eyelids. That tissue includes some of the muscles that support our eyelids. Fluid might also accumulate.

Apparently, some people resort to hemorrhoid cream to address eye bags, and perhaps they find it handy at the other end, too, as prescribed. Cool compresses can help, and the desperate and brave might opt for eye surgery, but skillful application of makeup can also hide a multitude of sins—and years.

Suit Up

Fortunately, there actually are quite a few basic ways to protect and rejuvenate your skin, which (fun fact!) is your body's largest organ.

Start inside: Drinking plenty of water moisturizes you from the inside out. Fish oil can also help with this. If you are drinking Reverse Osmosis-treated water, be sure to replenish the minerals that RO removes by adding electrolytes.

Pamper your outside, too: Use warm, not hot, water to bathe or shower. Then pat rather than rub yourself dry. Patting is easier on the skin and leaves some dampness that you can seal in with moisturizer.

Frequent moisturization seems too easy to be helpful, but it actually makes a big difference. I live in a dry place and my skin laps up lotion. I used to grumble about it until my doctor reminded me: "When a practice you resent actually makes a difference, you'll be glad to do it." Moisturizing has fallen firmly in that category for me.

Moisturizing also helps conceal blemishes, reduce dryness and oiliness, and helps even skin tones. That becomes more important than ever as we age and our skin gets blotchier.

There are lots of great moisturizing creams, including topical retinol ones that can help restore your skin's elasticity and thicken the collagen that helps firm skin.

Just massaging moisturizer into your skin helps by stimulating blood circulation and new cell growth. Such a great invitation for some luxurious pampering disguised as health care!

Going out? Wear sunscreen and cover up. And what the heck, go with it! Get some huge sunglasses with ample rhinestones and a sunhat with a large brim and learn to glide silently. Why yes, you *are* a classic movie star or maybe an international spy.

As for the sun's "deadly rays," ideally choose a lotion with an SPF of at least fifteen for daytime to prevent premature lines and wrinkles. There are also some tinted moisturizer/sunscreen combinations that give you makeup, lotion, and sun protection all at once.

Vitamins are a plus, too; A and B5 are good for increasing firmness and building moisture levels; C and E protect new skin and fight skin damage.

Radical Reinforcements

Okay, they aren't really radical, but there are other things you can do for your skin. Radio frequency, ultrasound, infrared, and lasers might tighten skin modestly by targeting the fibrous bands that attach skin to muscle, and some skin firming and tightening creams seem to work. Scientists are still seeking the Holy Grail that helps rebuild the protein in skin that governs elasticity. But at least they are still looking.

Collagen and protein supplements come in various forms, including pills, powders, and creams. They've worked for me, but your mileage may vary.

And then there are anti-aging products. Two main types are antioxidants and cell regulators. Antioxidants are rich in vitamins C, B, and E, and work more to prevent wrinkles than reverse damage, although they may reduce redness and inflammation, which will make skin healthier.

Cell regulator creams and lotions contain peptides, retinols, tretinoin, or growth factor ingredients to stimulate collagen production that helps firm neck and face skin.

You can also try laser peels as well as ultrasound and microneedling, which stimulate protein production in deeper layers to make skin firmer. If you're really serious (or desperate, conditions that may overlap) there are always injectables (botulinum toxin, various fillers to help minimize wrinkles, and more)—or the big plunge of getting a facelift.

As for the baths, moisture massaging, and other skin care, so what if you feel great doing it? Perhaps that sort of self-care is one of the *benefits* of aging.

Read the Label!

Even if it means carrying a pair of readers or even a magnifying glass with you, it's worth reading labels. Some manufacturers craftily label moisturizers that contain sunscreen (and no other active ingredients) as "anti-aging." It's not really deceptive—as we've covered, wearing sun protection is one of the best ways to keep skin in good shape. But compared to creams including more advanced—and, usually, more expensive—ingredients, that bargain moisturizer might not be what you hoped.

"I'll Be Right Back"

Some aging challenges affect men more than women (see "Hair Today"), but we all seem to spend more and more time running to or sitting on the john because our kidneys just aren't performing like they used to.

That's because, over time, kidney tissue and function decline, along with the nephrons that filter waste material from our blood. Kidney blood vessels also harden, causing them to filter more slowly. Our bladder's walls change, too: their tissues lose their elasticity so our bladders can't hold as much urine. (I'm trying to determine at this point if I'm depressed or just have to pee.)

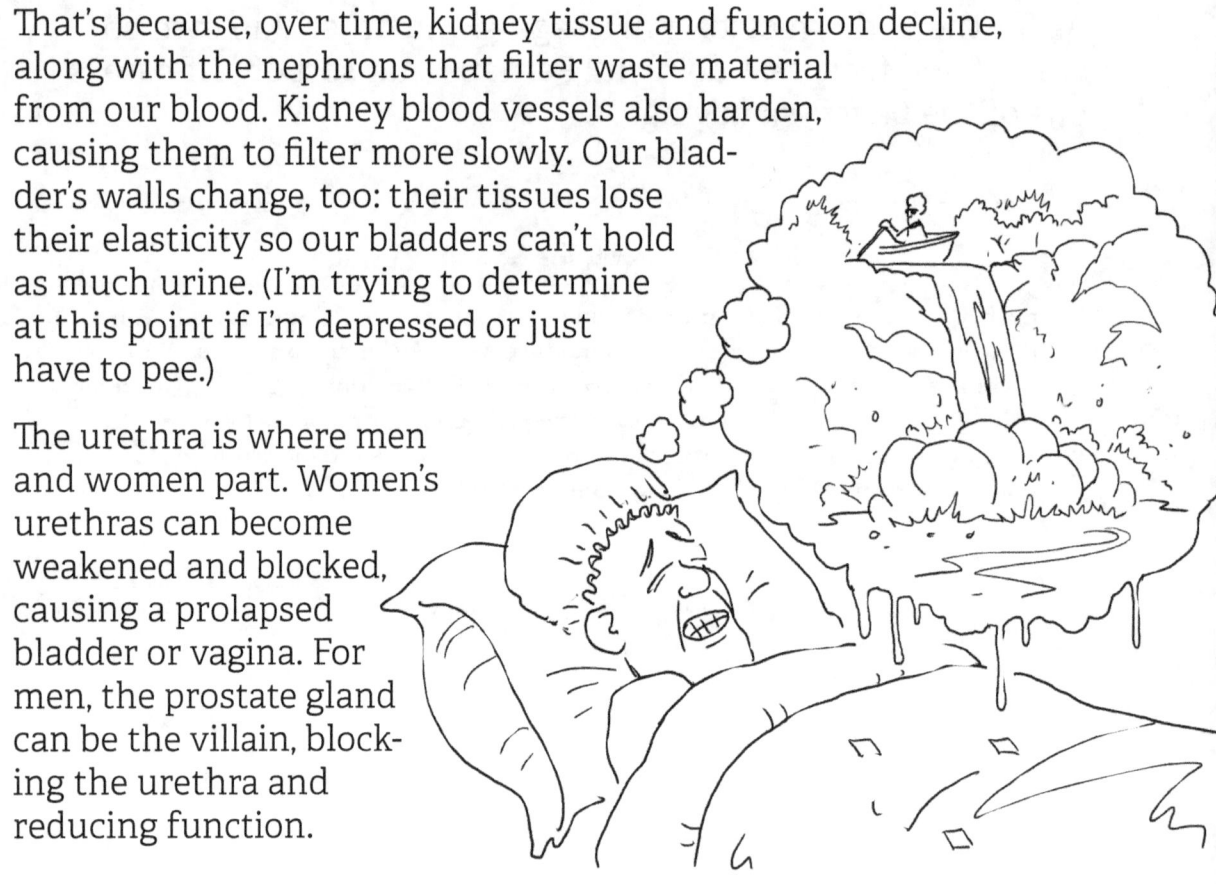

The urethra is where men and women part. Women's urethras can become weakened and blocked, causing a prolapsed bladder or vagina. For men, the prostate gland can be the villain, blocking the urethra and reducing function.

These problems send us looking for solutions, of which there are many, most of which you can learn about watching cable TV at two a.m. Perhaps that explains why some fancy hotels put a television in the bathroom—and maybe it's worth trying at home!

Whether bladder leakage can be addressed by the offerings of a retired athlete now starring in these late-night offers, there are things you can do. Avoid the usual suspects (tobacco, caffeine, and alcohol, as well as excess weight) and embrace pelvic floor, or Kegel, exercises to head off bladder leaks.

If they are done right for about three months, you can regain control of your muscles and—bonus!—improve your sex life.

This sounds like a win without having to relinquish your name, address, and credit card number to a company that will undoubtedly expose you to the myriad scams and semi-scams targeting anyone who regularly orders from television ads.

Necklines Never in Style

I once thought that an awful lot of older women had had major neck surgery. It looked like they'd practically had their heads cut off! Then my own neckline appeared, and despite some memory challenges, I definitely would have remembered nearly having my head severed.

It turns out they—we—had developed a different type of neckline than the ones on our shirts. This one is never in style. These necklines appear because our necks have thinner skin than our faces, and the platysma (the flat muscle surrounding the front of the neck) pulls apart and rolls into bands.

And while we older folks may be more inclined to develop neck lines, also known as neck bands, now even younger people who spend a lot of time staring at screens are developing a crease similar to that in a piece of paper. Genetics and weight gain don't help, either.

The result is those charming necklines and the alarming "turkey neck," which sounds as appalling as it looks.

But there are some things you can do. Most simple: keep your shoulders back and chin up to avoid creating creases. Retinol and sunscreen help, too.

Once the creases appear, though, you might want to try microneedling, which encourages your body to build collagen to repair the tiny holes and create smoother, brighter skin. More aggressive: radio frequency, or RF. Botulinum toxin and dermal fillers can also help.

And then there is your growing collection of snazzy (just using that word dates me, but I like it too much to resist) scarves . . .

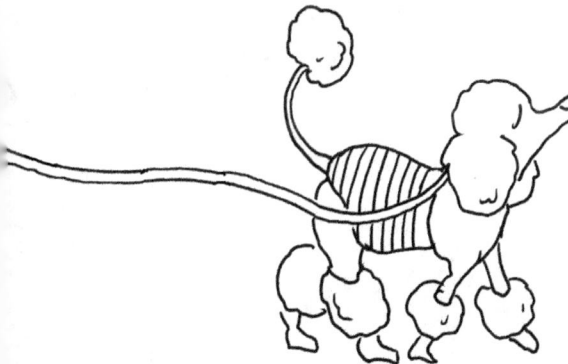

Hair Today

What happened to my husband's incredible russet mane? I still love him and what's left of his sexy, now silvery hair, but there's no question that he, like other males, suffers more hair loss than women. (No gloating, ladies. We have our own problems.)

We typically lose fifty to 100 hairs each day throughout our lives but don't notice because new hair is growing in at the same time. But plenty of things conspire to affect our hair. Number one, as you might have already guessed, is aging.

We are definitely at the mercy of our predecessors when it comes to male (and female) pattern baldness, but hormonal changes, medications, supplements, stress, poor nutrition, and radical hairstyles and hair treatments can also contribute.

It's no surprise that some hair loss has to do with the male hormone testosterone, which men also lose as they age when the chemical DHT, or dihydrotestosterone, breaks down testosterone.

It causes individual hair follicles to shrink and lose their ability to regenerate new hair.

Then, of course, is how our hair changes texture and turns gray. The change in texture is attributable to a loss of density and diameter as well as the usual wear and tear imposed by life.

We owe the gray to our melanocyte cells making less melanin, which creates the pigment. As we all know, color is easily addressed whether we are just trying to choose a color that will pass as God-given (you know, like makeup, which we are always told will make us look natural) or a wild orange, purple, or magenta that declares our defiance. My former hairdresser never discussed my gray hair, which she knew I wouldn't color, but simply referred to it as "sparkly." I can go with that.

Admittedly, gray and white hair looks better on some people than others, but if we have to live with it, let's celebrate it. Some older folks go wild with purple, blue, or green hues which can make a statement without saying a word.

Muscle Misfire

While I'd never claim to having been athletic as a kid and young adult, I was far from sedentary; I hiked, sailed, swam, played volleyball and hide-n-seek. I was fit, trim, and had no problem with my weight. Then one day I woke up and discovered that my body had been exchanged for that of a weakling. What the heck?!

I quickly discovered that, even if you never had to work out before, as you age, you need to exercise just to *maintain* your body. This was a deeply sad and life-changing discovery for me. I now spend hours stretching, lifting, bending, leaping, and rolling simply to stay in one place physically. No wonder no one told us—this alone might have tempted me to end it all early.

Now that I've accepted the reality, though, I'm embracing my spandex-clad self if for no other reason than dissipating into a blob is not the way I'd like to go. The good news: regardless of age, the human body responds to regular exercise, and there are a lot of health benefits to entice you to work out.

Indeed, it has been a too-well-kept secret that the number and size of muscle fibers simply decrease with age. Studies have shown that an average human body loses more than six pounds of lean muscle every decade during middle age—most, apparently, from sitting around doing nothing. (I would like to know where those pounds go. They certainly are not deducted from the number we see on the scale, yet another one of nature's cruel jokes.)

The muscles most affected are the "fast twitch" ones built for short, powerful bursts of energy, which explains how they deteriorated without you doing a thing. (Because you may be wondering, there are slow-twitch muscle fibers, too. They are built for endurance activities like long-distance running or biking.)

Once again—back to our recurring and sometimes annoying theme—exercise makes a difference. Specific workouts, like fast lifting, box jumps, jump squats, and kettle bell swings help build those fast-twitch muscles, but they all fall under the heading of moving and challenging our bodies to stay active and supple.

If you're like me, and I know I am, it really helps to have accountability to do all of this exercise whether you go to a gym, have a trainer come to you, or use an app or video on a regular basis.

The Knee Bone's Connected to the . . .

It seems that aging inflicts its own indignity on each part of our body. Bone density, for instance, begins to decline after age forty, and the pace accelerates when you reach fifty. That bone loss makes us more prone to fractures and osteoporosis, which is why Aunt Harriet (and Aunt Harriets everywhere) broke her hip.

Fortunately, weight-bearing exercise is particularly good for keeping bones healthy and strong. Pay attention, too, to your calcium and vitamin D levels, and avoid tobacco and too much alcohol.

If you are beginning to notice that exercise seems like a popular solution to many aging issues, you get bonus points for a quick mind. Yes, it's a recurring theme, and while it may not be what you were hoping for ("The solution? Eat chocolate!"), it beats surgery and pills in oh-so-many ways.

Say Can You See

It's clear: Your eyesight becomes worse as you age. It's one of the most common effects of aging, and why we almost all end up using reading glasses by the time we reach our forties or fifties. It makes sense when you realize that the lenses of our eyes lose flexibility as we age, making it more difficult to focus on close objects.

After a lifetime of sun, wind, high blood pressure, and other inflammatory influences, our eyes also dry out, meaning we produce fewer tears and more burning, stinging, and sometimes, oddly, watery eyes.

If you're on the other side of sixty and are wondering why you crave more light to see and read, you aren't imagining things. As we age, the little muscles around our pupils make them smaller. That's why people in their sixties need three times more light to read comfortably than those a third their age. Now that I have magnifying glasses in almost every room, I'm ready to start researching headlamps.

And what about those specks? Called floaters, they appear when the fluid behind an eye's lenses begin to break down. They're not fireworks, and they aren't serious—unless you get a shower of them with light flashes. Those aren't fireworks, either, but they are a good reason to see an eye doctor as soon as possible.

Sometimes floaters are caused by posterior vitreous detachment, a common age-related eye problem caused by the vitreous gel that fills your eyeball separating from your retina, which detects light and turns it into visual images. PVD can cause you to see black or white specks, flashes of light, or shadows over four to six weeks. If the gel completely separates from your retina, what you see may evolve. An ophthalmologist can answer questions and make sure what you are seeing isn't harmful but just your own private fireworks display brought to you by Aging, Inc.

Cataracts, a film that can develop on eye lenses, are yet another gift of aging. By the time we reach eighty, more than half of us will have had them, although they aren't always detectable. If objects seem blurry, lights seem too bright, and colors seem faded, you'll want to check in with an optometrist or ophthalmologist.

The good news is that cataract surgery is safe and common. Why just restore your vision, though, when you can actually improve it during this surgery. It's gotten so sophisticated, I've overheard my friends discussing what "package" they were getting as if shopping for a cruise.

The Eyes Have It

Macular degeneration is another "gift" of aging that most of us can do without. Often called age-related macular degeneration, or AMD, it primarily affects the macula, which is the central part of the retina, which governs sharp, central vision. Macular degeneration is a leading cause of vision loss for the over-sixty crowd and can make everyday tasks like reading, driving, and recognizing faces difficult. Although there's no cure, there are treatments. You definitely want to consult a doctor to determine whether you have "dry" or "wet" AMD and how to best treat it.

Whether changes in vision are precipitated by heredity, dry weather, or smoking, nearly all age-related vision changes can be medically treated. Presbyopia, which causes our eye lenses to be less flexible, can be addressed with surgery. Over-the-counter artificial tears or gels help dry eyes. Eating fish high in omega-3 fatty acids (salmon, tuna, and halibut) as well as flax and chia seeds can also help keep eyes from drying.

Wearing sunglasses and a brimmed hat protects eyes, too. Quitting smoking and eating healthy foods not only reduce blood pressure but also help keep eyesight healthy. If you spend a lot of time on the computer, try looking away every twenty minutes for at least twenty seconds to give your eyes (and mind) a rest.

That's a good time to stand up and stretch, too. Time flies easily, so I set a kitchen timer for twenty minutes. When the buzzer goes off, it reminds me to stand up, breathe, and stretch—and focus on what I'm feeling to give my brain a break from thinking.

As for my compromised eyesight, I'm grateful it makes everyone look a little softer around the edges—and that I look that way to them, too.

Now Hear This

All that loud music we enjoyed as teenagers is now indeed coming back to haunt us. (Yes, I heard you, Mom.)

While some age-related hearing loss is caused by genetics and earwax, we probably did screw up our hearing going to all of those rock concerts—although I'm still glad I saw Jefferson Starship with their four semi trucks of amplifiers. Wear and tear affects the inner ear and auditory nerve, making it harder to tolerate loud sounds, discern high-pitched sounds like doorbells, and even understand what people are saying.

Tinnitus doesn't help, either. While generally thought of as ringing, it can manifest as clicking, roaring, and other disarming sounds. A symptom rather than a disease, tinnitus can check in and out of each or both ears. It can be caused by earwax, high blood pressure, and other issues, so it's worth mentioning to your doc.

And don't fear the audiologist (you might want to look out for the Reaper, though—he's a much scarier dude). Hearing aids have come a long way. They're now so sophisticated you often can't even see them, and they have controls that let you adjust sound levels as you enter a room or even do it for you automatically.

Recent research suggests a connection between dementia and hearing, so this is one health decline you definitely don't want to ignore.

Speak Up

Your biceps and hamstrings aren't the only muscles affected by aging. The muscles in our throats and jaws can also weaken. They then conspire with tissues and glandular changes to make our voices hoarse, breathy, or shaky as well as causing them to vary in pitch, usually higher in men and lower in women. Aging can affect the larynx and vocal cords when the muscles atrophy or shrink. When we're about sixty, our mucus membranes thin while connective tissues stiffen.

This has all the earmarks of a mutiny.

A lack of use doesn't help. My husband has ridden his motorcycle across the United States a half-dozen times and has found that, after a couple of days without talking to almost anybody, his voice decides it's on vacation, too.

Maintaining your voice is the same as so many other parts of your life (and body): Use it or lose it. Singers don't just walk out on the stage and sing; they take voice lessons and use those funny phrases and silly scales to limber up.

If singing doesn't appeal to you, recite poetry, take up public speaking, create videos, sing in the shower, or otherwise exercise your vocal cords without getting too crazy loud or whispery soft.

Hang On

One of the early warning signals that my body and I were not tracking evenly was when I realized I could not open jars anymore. Sure, I equipped my kitchen with rubber grippers and on occasion resort to denting a metal lid with a knife handle or tapping it on a hard surface, but there is no question that both my hand and finger strength seemed to vanish overnight.

Apparently, without consulting the afflicted (that's us), our bodies tend to lose hand strength after the age of sixty, which apparently is a very dangerous age (who knew!). In fact, a common change also caused by age is a 25 to 45 percent reduction of muscle mass, and some of those muscles are in our hands.

Once again, using them helps, which is why you see so many of us squeezing rubber balls. Laugh all you want; it works.

Wear and Tear (No Warranty)

When you're a teenager you feel immortal. Not only will you live forever, you have no clue that all of the bike crashes, death-defying falls, twenty-four-hour party marathons, earsplitting concerts, frostbite from falling asleep in the car after a rough night of carousing, and other insults to your system *will* come back to haunt you.

Yet reality dawned for a half-million people in a UK study. It found that past fractures, especially involving the spine and hips, can lead to chronic widespread body pain later in life.

On the bright side, it can also contribute to being able to predict when it's going to rain. When your bones heal, a callus forms where the fracture occurred. That callus eventually hardens to become new bone tissue that is, sadly, not only not as strong as the original bone, it's also more sensitive to changes in atmospheric pressure.

It isn't only bones, though. As we age, our tissues degenerate, which affects the structure and function of our vital organs. So, yes, we are literally falling apart. Unless you've had frostbite, which can result in increased sensitivity to cold, numbness, stiffness, and pain in the affected area as you age. In that case you are mummifying in place.

Would we have done anything differently when we were younger to avoid the pain and creaking of old age? Yeah, no, probably not. Immortality is forever! (Until it isn't.)

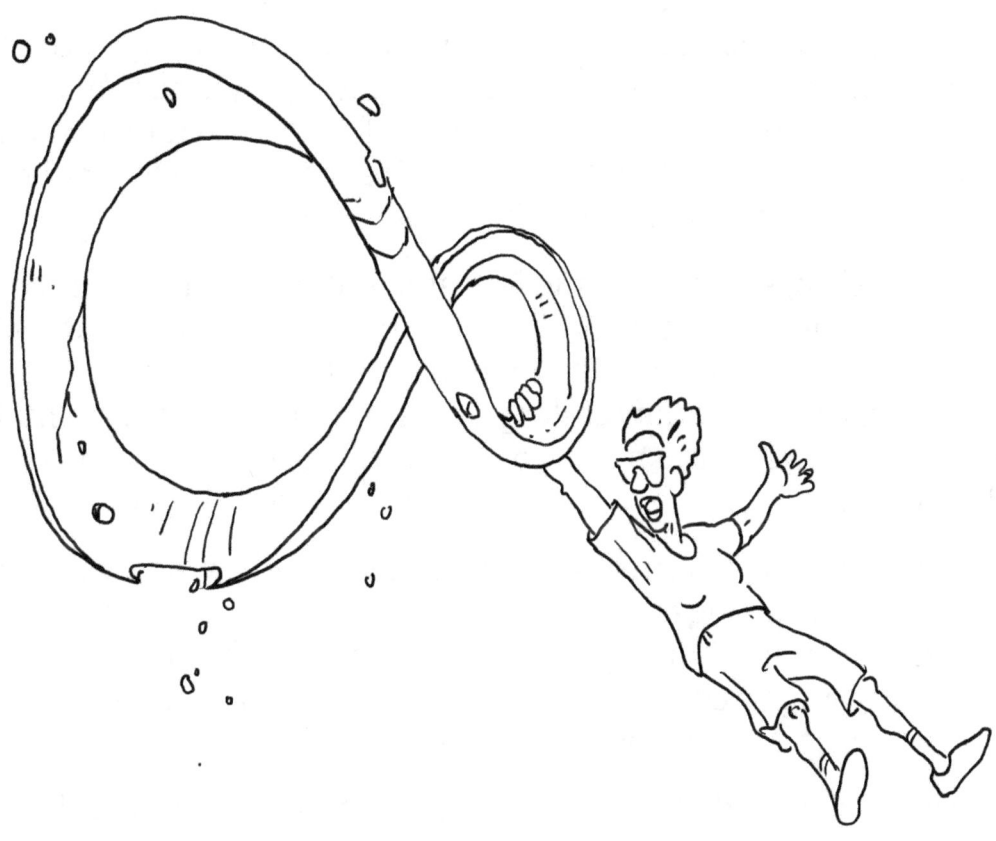

Can't, Not Won't

It was sobering to discover that I now sometimes cannot do things I used to be able do without a thought.

It's not that I don't want to do these things. It's that I can't.

I used to think people got smarter as they aged and simply began parsing what was worth doing and what wasn't (and there *is* something to that). My unfortunate discovery was that sometimes it isn't that I can choose what to focus on—in fact, I want to do it all, which makes it difficult—it's that my body just doesn't have the stamina or strength it needs to bounce back.

As our cells age, they become less efficient and functional. We can blame our parents—it actually could be in our genes—but cells also are dramatically affected by our lifestyles. Too much "too much" (toxins, infections, allergens, stress, sun, pollution, smoking, poor diet, and too much food) can release free radicals that damage mitochondria, which are what create energy in our cells.

Not only can we just not do what we used to do, what we do manage to do takes longer. Our minds don't process as fast or as fully, and the combination of physical and mental "off-ramping" can be frustrating. It can help to realize that it's not personal but just part of aging. It really does happen to us all.

There is a good side to this slowing, which is the opportunity to be more present in the moment, more patient with ourselves and others, and more aware of what is going on around us. It becomes more about "being" than "doing". It's one reason grandparents can be great with kids: They have the perspective, patience, and time to really *be* with their grandchildren, often more so than when they were parents.

As for the physical side, there is hope, but it requires your participation—once again, you need to move. You can increase your heart rate and lung activity with aerobic and endurance activities like spirited walking, biking, dancing, jogging, and swimming. Now *that's* more like living!

Why All the Buffets in Sun City Are Full at Five P.M.

It took me a while to figure out that my body processes food best at midday. So much for "breakfast like a king, lunch like a queen, and dinner like a pauper."

It *is* a good idea to start the day with a healthy meal including protein for an initial burst of energy as well as to eat plenty of protein through the day. As we age, though, our organs, including our digestive tracts, may not work as well. Your gut's muscles get stiffer, weaker, and less efficient, and new cells don't replace the old ones like they used to. So, call it "linner," "dunch," or stick with "dinner," but if you're having trouble digesting food in the evenings, eat earlier.

It also helps to eat smaller, fiber-rich meals, drink plenty of fluids, and avoid spicy and fatty foods.

So get your five p.m. reservations at your favorite restaurant—another bonus of aging since early spots are easier to get! Whatever time you eat, pay attention to what your body will and won't put up with, and enjoy every bite.

We Make a Lot More Noises

Apparently, many young men do not realize that women fart. By the time they've celebrated a lot of anniversaries (perhaps with one or more partners, but hey) they've heard the whole symphony. Farting, coughing, hacking, belching, and the occasional snort compose the soundtrack of most aging peoples' lives. Fortunately, our hearing is going, too, and hopefully our tolerance of each other's foibles has been leavened by empathy.

Of course, our body chimes in other ways, too. At a recent yoga class for women over fifty, we all stood up to a chorus of co-ordinated cracks. It's no surprise a bunch of yoga enthusiasts would find the funny in it. Indeed, at every opportunity, we all might as well laugh.

In fact, joint noises aren't necessarily bad. As my personal trainer points out, "If it hurts, it's bad. If it just makes noises, it might even be good." The popping is caused by our cartilage wearing away as we age, leaving rough edges that make noise as they rub against each other (kind of

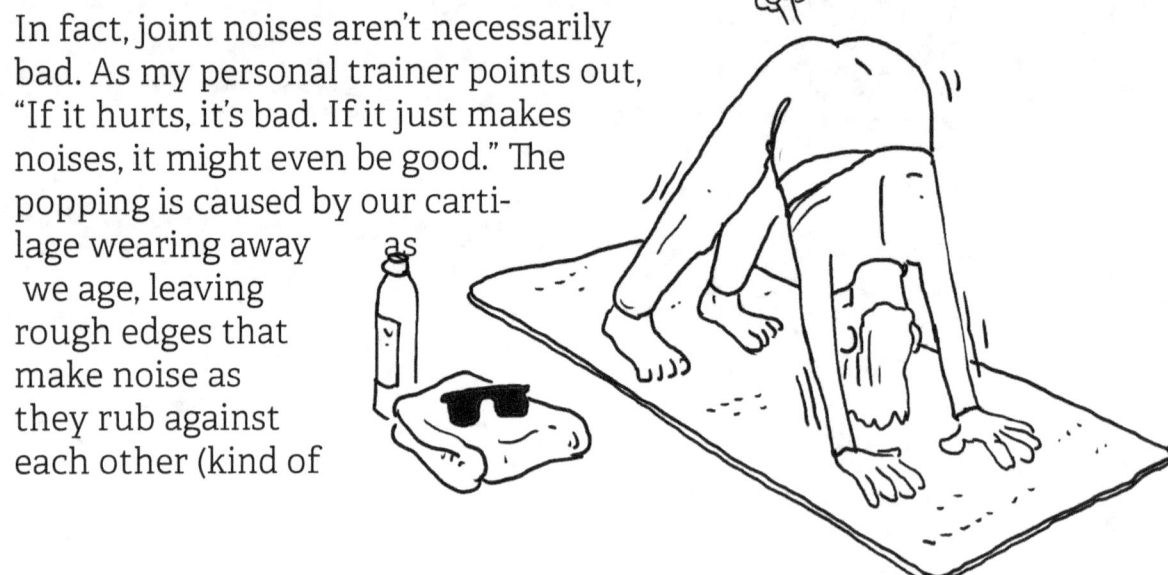

like my cat, but purring this ain't). Popping and clicking can also be caused by tight muscles and tendons rubbing over the bone, something a little healthy stretching can quiet.

Knuckles pop due to the compression of nitrogen gas, which naturally forms in our joints, being released. And this is one time Mom was wrong: Cracking them won't make your knuckles bigger or cause arthritis. But it might have stopped you from cracking them on purpose (or made you do it more just out of spite.)

To reduce the cacophony, the usual advice applies: *Move.* The synovial fluid in your joints cushions bone ends and reduces friction, so get it flowing!

But joints might not provide the only music from the orchestra . . .

Sex Isn't What It Used to Be

Remember when you wanted to be an adult so you could stay up late, sleep in, and have sex as close to twenty-four hours a day as possible?

Well, guess what else wears out?

It's not all bad. Some older people have more fun than when they had to hide their pleasure from parents or their own kids. And there are no worries about getting pregnant! Too, they may better understand and be able to discuss with a partner what they like. (Please feel welcome to take a break to fantasize or practice here.)

But some of our parts do make it challenging. Women's vaginas may shorten and narrow, while the vaginal walls can thin and stiffen right when lubrication is possibly waning as well.

Menopause is no help, either. Did someone say, "hot flashes," "lack of sleep," and "mood changes"?

But this is one time that men also bear the ravages of aging. It's when erectile dysfunction rears (or doesn't rear) its head, reducing the ability to have and keep as firm or large an erection. Some medications can contribute to problems, but so can being overweight, smoking, too much alcohol and not enough exercise. Decreased testosterone also contributes and can be addressed by a medical professional with shots or pellets. PDE5 inhibitors like that little blue pill can help by increasing blood flow to the penis.

These medications, like sildenafil or tadalafil, can improve erections by increasing blood flow to the penis. Other treatments like pelvic floor, or Kegel, exercises or vacuum erection devices might help, too. There are all definitely topics to discuss with a medical professional as well as your partner.

So, enjoy the extra adult time. Use whatever enhancements, tools, programs, and discoveries to make your sex life rich and fun. You've earned it. And now no one is going to question or shame you.

Balancing Act

When I was growing up, an older person falling in the shower or breaking a hip cued the first bars of a funeral dirge. The end was seldom far away. I not only never thought it would happen to me, I also never considered why older people fall.

It is, as you might have suspected, a conspiracy. Some medications, as well as alcohol, diabetes, heart disease, stroke, or problems with your inner ear, vision, thyroid, nerves, and blood vessels can cause dizziness and other balance problems.

You can address some of these ills individually and also can work with a physical therapist or other professional to identify movement exercises that might help address balance disorders.

Should I mention not walking in the dark and wearing sensible shoes? You're right—I didn't think you needed me to tell you that.

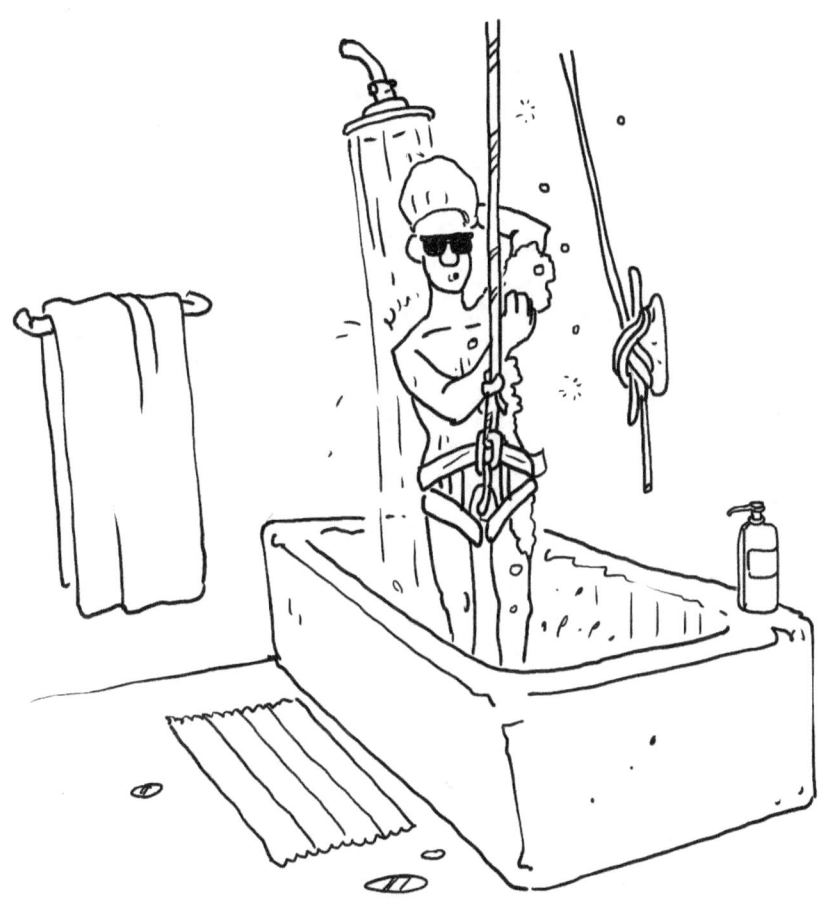

PART 3

THINK ABOUT
THE GOOD THINGS

The hardest working man in show business, James Brown, had it right when he said, "Think about the good things." And there are good things about aging.

It's not just about thinking positively, although that actually is a proven technique for improving your life. Studies have shown that smiling releases helpful body chemicals including neuropeptides, which fight stress, as well as neurotransmitters including the feel-good chemical dopamine, antidepressant serotonin, and pain-relieving endorphins.

Smiling is infectious, in that it makes people around you happier, too. Everyone in our neighborhood waves to everyone else, which helps us connect with other humans, a Good Thing.

Also good: Aging brings us positive results that outweigh what we may lament losing. They may be fewer in number, but they are more important and powerful than the annoying gnats of negativity . . .

It's Easier to Recognize the Small Stuff

The arc of life offers plenty of opportunity to see stuff large and small, short range and long. When you look at the entire span, you begin to see that losing that volleyball game in sixth grade was not, after all, the end of the world.

Nor is it now the worst thing you can imagine.

Somehow, we manage to make it through the good and the bad, regardless of how severe the latter may be. As we shuffle along, if we're paying attention, we're able to discern where whatever is going on fits into the big picture. We know what highs and lows look like and how this situation compares to a lifetime of experience. Almost certainly no downer is as bad as it seems at the time. As someone once reminded me when I made a mistake, "No one died."

Consciously stopping to think about a thorny issue helps us to make the right decision. Sometimes sorting it out comes down to asking, "If I were looking back ten years from now, what would I wish I'd done?" The answer can come quickly and be amazingly obvious from that perspective.

So many things that we thought we could never survive, well, we survived them. And that helps us realize that we can handle a lot more than we might have imagined. Viewing the bad times in context with the extended span of our lives lets us do exactly that.

Here's to our arc!

We're More Inclined to Speak Honestly

A lot of older people get increasingly blunt as they age. With the clock ticking, are they concerned about wasting time beating around the bush?

That bluntness might be caused by bunions or arthritis, or, frankly, could it just be that older people no longer care what others think? Or that it's high time someone actually says what everyone has been thinking?

Whatever encourages people to be more honest as they age, it's one reason I've always liked older people. Now that I apparently am one, it's my responsibility to set an example for the next generation to tell it like it is. Yes, I am the auntie your mother wishes you wouldn't visit.

We Get Better at Picking Friends

Most of us have a few close longtime friends, maybe even a life-long friend. Many of us have had to learn how to pick friends who will fill the role they didn't know they were auditioning for. Then there's the fact that we change over time, which means that our needs shift, too.

Still, as we age, we learn that we don't want to hang out with a drama queen (or king), a Chatty Cathy, or perhaps a Teeny Tears who wets and cries.

Unless you're too picky, you will hopefully end up with friends who laugh at the same things you do, enjoy the same movies and music, and like the same food and fun. And then there are those people who don't care about any of those things but care about you.

Too, we learn that not all friends need to be lifelong ones. Friendships may cushion our ride through life the whole way, but there's nothing wrong with discovering we may have different stops on the bus route of life. If we're aware and fortunate, we're able to wave goodbye with dignity and goodwill.

These discoveries don't dilute the value of friendships, they just make it worthwhile to pick our friends carefully. Thank goodness it can get easier, especially if we're paying attention to what we want and need now for ourselves and from others.

We Finally Like the Music in the Grocery Store

I speak for myself and many other Baby Boomers and Gen X'ers who used to cringe in elevators and grocery stores.

Now there's no more "Down by the Lazy River" or lounge versions of "Girl from Ipanema." Instead, the invisible Musical Powers That Be play the Beatles, Tom Petty, Credence Clearwater Revival, The Doobie Brothers, and even Steely Dan. Gen X babies are getting used to occasionally hearing the White Stripes or Jane's Addiction in the dairy aisle.

Is the grocery store getting hipper or am I just fortunate that the person picking the music is now my age?

Since I don't live around elevators, I don't know if their music has also somehow magically become palatable, but I'm not sorry that I can now happily hum along in the soup aisle. And yeah, that's me belting out the chorus now and then.

What are they going to do, throw me out on Senior Savings Day?

Payback Time

When my mother was in her mid seventies she discovered senior discounts. Mom liked saving money, but for her it was really all about the hunt.

It turns out that a lot of businesses give discounts to people simply for living long enough. (In 1975, my grandfather lucked out with a loophole on this front. When he turned 96, the insurance policy he'd bought years before started paying him back. They've "fixed" that now.)

While many companies tout 10 or 15 percent savings for seniors, others will give you a break only if you ask. That's why Mom was forthright about asking for discounts. Her dentist may have laughed, but even that's a decent payoff.

We Shed the 'Shoulds'

At a certain point—usually one that sneaks up on you, like suddenly grasping that you're now your oldest relative—you realize you also are your own authority.

This is true even if you have a boss or a spiritual leader in your life. You can decide whether to attend a religious service or keep your job (well, pretty much).

But all those "shoulds" you grew up with ("You shouldn't stay up too late on a school night." "You should visit your Aunt Maude," whom you never liked. "You really shouldn't wear a flowered top.") now mean nothing.

Well, you might want to avoid certain consequences, especially ones relating to staying employed or alive, but that's your choice. As a grownup on the downward slope of the curve, it's OK to let the "shoulds" slide away where they may.

We Get Smarter

OK, maybe we don't get smarter as such, but it sure seems that way if we are paying attention.

So much can be learned if we are able to notice what is happening and why.

Is it something that has only happened once? Is it something that keeps happening? Does any way that we respond change the situation for the better or worse? What can we learn, and how can we use that experience to improve our lives and those around us?

Being able to analyze and assess what happens to us inevitably enables better—and calmer—responses. We all have this capability and many of us may be using it without even knowing.

As we analyze and assess, we can also heighten our intuition, if we can be quiet enough to tap into it and keep exercising our "intuition muscle," building skills that improve with time and experience.

If we nurture this powerful internal tool, our intuition will continue to improve, and that's definitely a good thing.

We're Expected to Celebrate Our Birthday Months

Sure, you can celebrate your birthday for a whole month when you're a kid (although you may have a hard time convincing anyone else to), but the extended celebrations happen naturally as you get older. People even bring it up, using it as a reason to get together.

As a mature adult you also have more friends who want to take you out to celebrate. Frankly, at some point, what else are birthdays good for? We won't all agree when it's time to celebrate a "milestone" age—for me it was when I turned twenty-six and my car insurance payment dropped—but any reason to celebrate and have fun is a good one.

Birthdays can be a handy annual excuse for a month of good times.

We Finally Like Naps and Baths

What is there about naps and baths not to like? I'm not sure, but when I was a kid, I fought them as if my future depended on it.

When I was young, I'd stamp my foot and insist, "I'm too old to take a nap!" Today I can't wait for my midday respite. While even lying down and reading for fifteen minutes helps, I've discovered that closing my eyes and surrendering to a timer to head off anxiety does wonders. Now I'm negotiating with myself for another fifteen minutes.

As for baths, their restorative powers are not all in your head. A warm bath can actually make your blood flow more easily and help oxygenate it by encouraging you to breathe more deeply and slowly, especially when the room is steamy. A hot bath or spa can even improve your immunity to bacteria, viruses, and other illness-causing nasties, which is why people often draw a bath when they are battling a cold or flu.

So see, we are maturing!

Less Close Shave

As teenagers, one of the first signs of maturing is the growth of new hair—under our arms, in our crotches, and on our legs. For females, It's often very exciting—until we find out we are, at least in Western culture, expected to remove it with a sharp blade. Then begins a protracted pursuit to eliminate every hair out of place, which is pretty much every one that is not coming out of the top of our heads.

While we lament so many other losses in aging, take heart that a drop in estrogen leads to one good thing: Our body hair becomes sparser and thinner. Mind you, we are only talking about legs and underarms here, because what may be happening on our heads and chins is not the best of news. It is, however, an edge aging women have over their male counterparts.

In addition to the changes that come with less estrogen, female skin thins more dramatically than mens'. We also lose subcutaneous tissue and our hair follicles get smaller, all of which results in finer, fuzzier hair. Or no hair. I haven't shaved my legs in more than a year. Sorry if that's TMI, but I'm not afraid to shout it from the rooftops. Yes, something to celebrate!

As for men, after the initial thrill of shaving a few nascent chin hairs, shaving can become an unwelcome daily chore. Fortunately, depending upon their jobs, men may be able to get away with the three-days-of-stubble look. And once you're retired, well, who says you have to shave at all?

If you are wondering whether the hair really shows up somewhere else instead, say sprouting from your chin or as a dapper moustache, I'm sorry to say that's likely the case. This is due to your testosterone levels rising. (Oddly both low and high testosterone can affect hair loss, which is why some people consider balding men potentially more virile.)

For women that volunteer sprouting isn't anything that can't be dispatched with a pair of great tweezers or a "lady moustache shaver." Whatever it takes with a minimum amount of pain and maximum removal helps keep this circus sideshow at bay.

What Goes Around Comes Around

When many of us were younger, we sneaked behind the metaphorical barn to smoke marijuana. It was expensive, full of seeds, harsh and, oh yeah, illegal, but we enjoyed the feeling it gave us.

Now that we've lived long enough that pot is legal in most U.S. states, we can toke openly. Or enjoy vaping, gummies, or several other ways to ingest it. And now that real research is being done into what it can do medicinally, we know ganja has benefits beyond feeling groovy. It may well help with glaucoma, anxiety, epileptic and other seizures, and lack of sleep, among many other conditions. Some research suggests marijuana may even be used to treat cancer because of its ability to reduce inflammation.

The best news about what some call a miracle drug is that serious research is being done enthusiastically by scientists, which means we can take certain types of pot for specific conditions.

No gloating, but this is one substance for adults only. Some research has shown that pot is not for teenagers, whose brains are still developing.

As a bonus, we already can enjoy the euphoric side effects that titillated us as kids—and make us care less about aches and pains.

We Pretty Much Do What We Want to Do

If you are at all paying attention as you age, you notice that you are good at some things, not so much at others. Certain things come easily to you, while others are a struggle. You enjoy some of them immensely, while others bore you to tears or make you angry.

That's led us to being able to live more selectively. Some things we have to do—like being able to eat, sleep comfortably, and pay our bills—but we can decide whether we have to finish reading a book we aren't enjoying or watch the rest of a movie that isn't likely to improve.

This sense of freedom isn't limited to wealthy people. Watch older people—that couldn't be us, so you know, people older than us—and notice how they can carve out a life that makes them feel the way they want to feel, no matter their socioeconomic status. They simply don't do things they don't want to do, whether it's using computers, wearing anything other than sweats, or bothering with lipstick.

Admittedly, some of this is due to the fact we can no longer do some of the things that we used to. Fortunately, though, we can make decisions about how we use our energy. Perhaps in that way we are forced to become smarter and work that way, too.

Change Is Good

Spending more time looking back than forward is an ominous sign for the future. It's critical that we embrace change as we wholeheartedly reject curmudgeonism.

Of course, everything was better Back Then! But that was then. Embracing what's going on now as well as looking ahead—regardless of the future being shrouded in the unknown—is critical to living.

As we age, we see remarkable change, most of which is good. We grandkids once asked my grandfather, who was still vital when he died at 101, about the most amazing thing he'd seen in his lifetime. He didn't mention light bulbs (which were invented in 1879, the year he was born), cars, airplanes, computers, or space travel.

He paused. We all leaned forward to benefit from his hard-won wisdom. He finally answered with his own question: "You know those steak houses where you can go and get a great cut of beef for $2.49?" To him, change was that every day, and everyday change was that amazing.

Incredible things are happening all around us. Consider the advances in medicine in the last fifty years. Humans are living in space. Women can now have checking accounts without having their husband's approval or signature. That "confirmed bachelor" uncle is no longer a mystery, and cars can go hundreds of miles on a simple electrical charge. Telephone calls can be made pretty much from anywhere to anywhere (wait—that may not be a good thing . . .).

A check can be magically deposited just by taking a photo of it. We can communicate with friends and family around the world for virtually no cost. I could go on, but we can see the astonishing advancements around us by taking a moment to think about them.

Of course, we face challenges aplenty. There always will be. But there's no turning back, so let's embrace the good around and ahead of us.

PART 4

BUT WHAT CAN WE DO?

If you haven't yet slit your own throat or jumped off a cliff, relax. There are actions you can take to counteract aging's sneak attacks.

These are doable things, too, not just instructions written for only the most devoted people who are willing to sacrifice everything good.

We can feel better. Here are some ways.

Dead or Alive

Perhaps our toughest challenge is our health. The march of time does not care one bit about how we envisioned our lives or how we abused ourselves when we were younger and immortal.

Since our bodies seem to be the most obvious target, both for wear and tear and for our remediation efforts, a little triage helps "divide and conquer."

That means learning what to address and what to accept.

Sometimes, we just have to live with a problem.

Other times, medical intervention is available, but the risks may be more than we are willing to take.

My husband taught me to look at some losses as potentially temporary. Whatever I now have to give up or do more of is "for now," acceptance tinged with hope. I can do it for now.

Lost muscle tone? I can accept that, but I need to address it, too, by working out. I can accept my hair is growing gray and *can* color it—if I want to. Instead, I'll celebrate my gray "sparkles." I guess if it grew *too* thin, I could wear a wig. Sometimes acceptance helps us embrace change.

When it comes to bodily care, triage requires ongoing assessment and negoti- a-
tion. Paying attention makes you your own best contributor to isolating and addressing any issue.

We can start with fundamentals:

1. Does it hurt?

2. How long has it been hurting or doing what it is doing?

3. What can be done about it?

4. Is this something I need to do? Or can or must someone else do it?

Calmly approaching health challenges will help us make decisions about what to do.

Some things we decide to accept, while others are worth working on by using weight training, yoga, walking, stretching, boxing, meditation, and more.

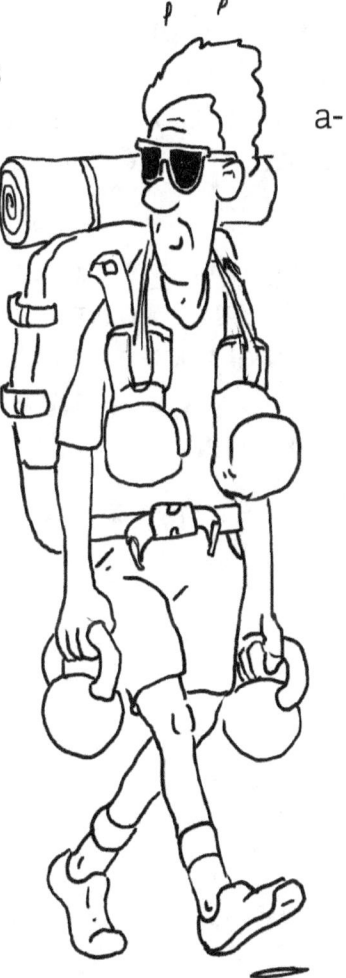

Other situations call for immediate attention—and a large number of issues confuse the hell out of us by not making the right path obviously clear.

Fortunately, we have been granted enough time to watch and decide whether to accept something as a part of our lives or to fight back. These choices may change as our lives advance, so we must continue to reassess our situation as time passes. But that beats running to the doctor every time something happens or just giving up.

It is probably worth it, by the way, to have doctors who may not be Doogies but are actually younger than you. They not only are likely better tapped into the latest information, they're also more likely to outlive you. That's important unless you like doctor shopping.

Too, it's important to . . .

Get a Move On

There is probably no single more valuable way to stay physically (and mentally!) healthy than to keep moving. You may have noticed this directive popping up repeatedly in this book, and it only underscores how important it is, whether you exercise alone or join a league or team.

Motion is lotion. Moving seems to remind our body parts, especially our joints, that we are, indeed, alive and need to keep them supple and healthy.

Weight-bearing exercise is particularly good for keeping bones healthy and strong. Even though I walk, stretch, use a foam exercise roller, and do yoga, weight training is my least favorite and most productive weekly activity. I can tell the difference it makes to torture myself lifting heavy objects and challenging my muscles.

So even though I don't actually like it, I keep practicing weight training and joke that I will probably die when a barbell traps me on the floor and prevents me from drinking and eating. While even then I might initially be happy about the resultant weight loss (although I would rather die having fabulous sex), I'll continue weight training just because of what I can see it doing for my body. As a bonus, it can help keep that fabulous sex happening.

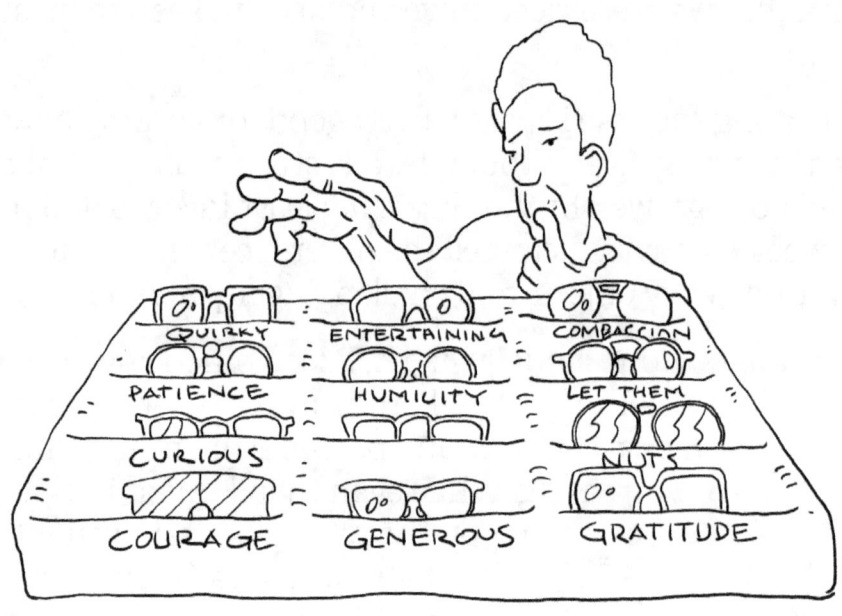

Attitude Is Everything

Of course, attitude is everything. We've been told that our whole lives. (Somewhere, Mom is smiling.)

Rather than box ourselves in with what we think people are supposed to do at our ages, it's possible to look at things in fresh ways and free ourselves from societal expectations.

As Max Planck, a theoretical physicist credited with discovering quantum physics, once observed (and author and teacher Wayne Dyer later popularized), "When you change the way you look at things, the things you look at change." It seems like your garden variety magical thinking, but oddly, it works. And it can change everything.

So can expansive thinking. Whenever I am stuck, I hark (I love harking, especially other than at Christmas) back to something I learned in a women's discussion group: Every challenge has at least ten solutions. Believing that expands my thinking far beyond what scant solutions I had initially dredged up. Suddenly I have new and fresh ideas, sometimes more than ten.

Whether I'm thinking about the past—rejecting guilt and embracing the lesson—living in the present, or considering the future, I know the importance of focusing on the positive. Anything else is a useless if not harmful distraction.

Eat It

As you've been reading this book, you've probably noticed that a loss of protein and collagen account for many of our aging bodies' challenges. Rather than go down the rabbit hole of where all that protein and collagen is going (China? Mars? Other places inappropriate to mention in a family book?), it's more productive to focus on what to do about it.

It's pretty simple: Consume more protein. My cardiologist directed me to consume twenty grams of protein every morning. My naturopath and my trainer say sixty to ninety grams for someone of my size, depending upon whether I'm trying to maintain or build muscle This focus on protein intake brought to my attention that I had actually been reducing my protein intake as I'd aged.

Now I start the morning with a protein shake, sometimes with some collagen powder since collagen, which you will recall also diminishes while aging, helps with hydration, elasticity, and wrinkle reduction. There are other sources of protein, including many types of food like nuts, eggs and Greek yogurt (which are healthier than protein bars and drinks). You might be surprised, as I was, how much of a difference it makes.

And while you're at it, drink more, preferably good, water. Whether you buy it or use a process like reverse osmosis (providing you add back in good minerals and electrolytes to the RO water), good water tastes better and goes down more happily. We've all read dire directives about the importance of drinking eight cups of water a day, but rather than focusing on quantity, focus on drinking as much as you can.

By the way, don't worry about drinking too much water unless you are emptying the water cooler. The chances of overdoing it or becoming a waterholic are unlikely at best. Drinking too much water overloads your kidneys, but not many people do so. Overconsumption of water causes serious symptoms including nausea, vomiting, and diarrhea, so you're not likely to ignore it.

Believing Is Being

Regardless of religious or spiritual upbringing, many people become more devout as their physical health decreases and the end of life nears. Some of us go deeper into our childhood beliefs, while others veer in a wildly new direction.

Some sort of belief system, whatever it may be, provides a place to rest our weary minds and bodies. Whatever the discipline, the practice is often faith. Faith that we are safe, that we are loved, that our lives have been worthwhile.

Some people find answers in places other than organized religion. You can laugh all you want at crystals and purple feathers, but if that gives you peace, I grant you room for it.

The father of my best childhood friend was a devout atheist. When he died, his family was unsure how to conduct a service without mentioning God or a higher power. My friend reached for one of his favorite books about nature, which was, when it came right down to it, his spiritual foundation.

It's certainly as good as any.

Abandon Expectations

How much pain is caused by things that never happen?

When I was about to marry my second husband, my father asked if I'd thought about the fact that he was eighteen years older than I. "Are you prepared to take care of an old man?" he wisely asked. I hadn't even considered the question. It didn't stop me from marrying him (he was a wonderful man and partner), but the worry would have been for naught as he died when he was just fifty-two (which now seems young to me). All that worry would have been wasted, as worry often is.

The villain in this case is expectations, which have never, as far as I can tell, helped anyone in any way.

Lao Tzu put it into perspective this way:

If you are depressed, you are living in the past.

If you are anxious, you are living in the future.

If you are at peace, you are living in the present.

Like shame and guilt, worry—often the offspring of expectations—has no benefit.

Shedding your expectations creates more room for peace and joy, which are always good in every way.

Put a Sock in It

Moaning and groaning is one habit to stop immediately. It can sneak up on you—one day you suddenly discover you have added a soundtrack to your daily life that sounds a lot like a haunted house.

If you find yourself "oomphing" as you stand up or sit down, stop it. Just stop it. All it does is make you sound old and feel worse.

It may take a while to break a habit you didn't know you'd developed. Start now. You'll feel better.

Please also shut the keyboard lid on the "organ recital." Our friends are aging, too, and we all are falling apart, but must we also talk about it all the time? The more we focus on our aches, pains, medications, and procedures, the worse we all feel.

So instead let's just watch cartoons and tell each other dirty jokes. That will make us laugh, which increases oxygen to our hearts, lungs, and muscles, and encourages our brains to increase the endorphins that both improve mood and reduce physical pain. Laughter reduces stress and anxiety, boosts the immune system, and calms the autonomic nervous system, which regulates involuntary processes including heart rate, blood pressure, digestion, sexual arousal, and more.

Interestingly enough, the body apparently can't discern between real and fake laughter, so all of those benefits are available even if nothing seems funny. That leads my friend Johnny to fake laugh every morning as he drinks his coffee, giving him a positive start to his day. So, what's not to laugh about?

Speaking of which, have you heard the one about . . .

Even if you have, you might have forgotten it or might just choose to laugh at it again.

Sex? Yes!

All of this urging to move your body sounds an awful lot like exercise. And yes, of course, exercise is probably required no matter what.

The good news? A great way to move is to have sex. The joints forget they're sore and your muscles suddenly recall their glory days (or close enough). It sometimes calls for creativity or "assistive devices" (there—doesn't that sound medicinal?!).

Some folks find that any combination of factors like comfort with yourself and your partner, no longer needing to worry about pregnancy, and getting past the embarrassment or sex negativity so many of us grow up with can lead to having even more fun than in our younger days. Or at least, different fun.

No one is filming (wait, they aren't, are they?), so don't worry if you don't look like Pamela and Tommy Lee. Screw up, fall down, laugh. You are not being graded.

And sex offers other important benefits, too. For men, ejaculating helps keep the juices moving, which may be particularly important when it comes to prostate health. Some people believe sex helps reduce the chance of prostate cancer. For women, orgasms can boost heart health, strengthen the immune system, and provide pain relief. Even if it just may be helpful—and there is no evidence it's harmful—why not do some original research? At the very least you'll have fun and sleep well.

Do you need more of an invitation? Dr. Ruth told us conclusively it's good for you—and she lived to the ripe old age of 96!

Nipping and Tucking

National treasure Dolly Parton is a walking contradiction and inspiration. No one has had more plastic surgery, worn more wigs or makeup, and yet is more authentic.

While I would never go to the extent Dolly does to, well, doll myself up, I admire her clear understanding of what she does and why she does it.

We don't have to go to such lengths, though, to buoy our spirits by getting a little, um, lift. If it will make you feel better to have your eyes lifted or your neck tightened, do it! The psychological impact can be huge.

Besides, you deserve to feel better about yourself.

Stay Curious

When we lose interest in the world, we age exponentially. Constantly following our curiosity, as author Elizabeth Gilbert so wisely advises, keeps us young. Our interests change, but our curiosity about how and why things work and how they can work better keeps us flexible.

Ray Kroc, the longtime CEO of McDonald's, said it well: "When you're green, you're growing. When you're ripe, you rot." If you find yourself telling the same stories over and over, most of them more than two decades old, it's a sign that you are stuck in the past.

Catch up! Even though there is an amazing abundance of ridiculous crap out there, you'll find plenty of things that interest—and may even delight—you. Know what subjects catch your fancy, whether it's advancements in space or sea travel, medicine or music.

Too, make an effort to remain relevant. This doesn't mean you have to like hip hop music or wear ripped jeans, but it does mean making an effort to know what is going on. Even if you don't understand it or like it, it's worth knowing what the world is up to. Read news—preferably from a variety of reliable sources so you can "triage the truth"—and keep up on the latest books, movies, and memes or at least have a handle on some of those things.

Don't just rely on outside sources, though. Awareness is our greatest ally. If we are aware of how our bodies—and minds—are responding to the world around us, we are more likely to make better decisions. It is easy to be distracted by tweets, posts, and friends' rants, but we ourselves are our own best witnesses.

Respect what you see and hear. You should probably leaven it with other input but trust your own observations. You might be surprised by what you already know.

Cool Shoes, Twinkly Tiaras, and Purple Hair

Since many of us are no longer consumed with finding a mate, why not make the most of expressing ourselves through our wardrobe. Or if we're looking for the right mate, that's even more important.

Perhaps your grandma paved the way after the 1930s by having a blue rinse, which made gray or white hair look less yellow. Now people aren't waiting until they have cotton candy hair to add a rainbow of color—not necessarily all at once, but if the mermaid look floats your boat, go for it.

A friend changed my life by giving me a tiara. At first I thought, "Cute, but what the heck am I going to do with this?" Then I discovered that tiaras must be sprinkled with magic fairy dust because—and this is true—when I wear it, I feel powerful. In public, people look at me like I'm crazy, which is probably accurate, but I don't care. Royalty is never unduly distracted by the little people.

Women aren't the only ones who feel newly free to fly their freak flags. You don't have to limit your rebellious streak to an aubergine lock in your mane, though. Anyone can wear cool shoes and choose glasses frames and statement jewelry that illustrates just who they are. As Oscar Wilde is credited with saying, "Be yourself; everyone else is already taken."

Celebrating your greatest assets also helps to distract from aspects you might not want to focus on. So, if it makes you feel good, flaunt it!

Be Silly

Is there anything that keeps us younger than being childlike? I plan to ride my loaded grocery cart to my car for the rest of my life. I like wearing a goofy hat, making faces at kids in other cars and at driverless Waymo cars with their whirring cameras, and doing other things that make other people laugh because it makes me laugh, too. That peels away the years.

It also helps set an example. When people see how much fun I'm having, they can't help but smile and maybe ride their grocery carts, too. I hope younger people see they don't have to be fuddy-duddies as they age. Being harmlessly crazy is a lot more fun.

Really Do Eat Dessert First

Why the heck shouldn't we start with the best part of the meal? Isn't this the ultimate reward for being a grownup? No matter how unhealthy it is, eating dessert first is a power move.

I'm usually well-behaved about eating meals with at least some redeeming healthy value, but every now and then popcorn or ice cream is enough.

There's no one around to say no, and I'd like to think that my grandpa is up there smiling at the good example he set.

ACKNOWLEDGMENTS

Thanks to these enthusiastic and intrepid souls for their input, feedback, contributions, assistance, encouragement, and patience, and for laughing in most of the right places as well as some new ones I didn't know yet were funny.

So many people helped over the years that it is impossible to thank them all here, but I appreciate them very much nonetheless. They've made my life better and, I hope others' lives, too.

My deepest thanks to the many wonderful souls who contributed to this book, especially (and, as someone whose last name starts with "W" in reverse alphabetical order), Kurt Wright, Laura Wilber, Oscar Wilde, Janet Whalen, Dr. Ruth Westheimer, Rachel Westheimer, May Westheimer, Irvin Westheimer, John Westheimer, Duffie Westheimer, Charles Westheimer, Bill Westheimer, Dr. Decker Weiss, Lao Tzu, Dr. Jim Tuggle and his crew, Cindy Tatu, Rebecca Samuelson, Rudy Schur, Connie Stocker, Pat Smith and the ladies of her magical Tuesday yoga class, Lainie Schimdt, Daniel Prendergast, Max Planck, Dolly Parton, Aiste Parmasto, Eddie Orton, J. Robert Orton, Gladys Orton, Claire Nullmeyer, Terry Nathan, Ellenor Mueller, Ellen Leibow, Dr. Michael Leff, Karen Leff, Elizabeth Lotspeich, Linda Kaplan, Sarah Kriehn, Ray Kroc, Lindsay Hyzer, Elizabeth Gilbert, Bela Fidel, Dr. Ramin Fathi, Christopher Dorris, the DJs at my local Fry's store, Mark Caron, Susan DeJong, Colleen Carmean, Heather Bachtel, James

Brown, Shawna Burkhart, Brian Burkhart, David Allen, Trudy Anand, and the members of my brilliant book club, Diane Silver, Jill Rubin, Carol Minchew, Ruth Landau (who provided fascinating comments), Christine Leva, Susan Hersker, Judith Engleman, Jennifer Eisel and Joyce Crawford.

I extend special shoutouts to Elizabeth Murfee DeConcini, Dino DeConcini, Eileen Szychoswki, Johnny Hamilton, Barbara McNichol, Ruth Landau, Judy Colbert, and Andrea Beaulieu for some especially insightful editorial input. Special thanks to my guiding lights in the development of this book, Marcella Smith and Mariah Bear.

This book would not be the same without Robert Chambers' inspired and delightful illustrations. He captured the energy of the book, peopling it with characters I might want to be friends with but whom I could, regardless, write entire stories about. They are as real as the issues we all face together.

Last and first, I thank my boundlessly patient husband, Kevin Caron, for this and so much more.

ABOUT THE AUTHOR

Mary Westheimer never intended to write this book. Somehow, though, a list that she kept for years grew. She blames everyone who laughed at her observations and contributed their invaluable experiences as well as their expertise for the book's existence.

She has written all her life, however, and previously penned one book, *The History of Kappa Alpha Order,* for which a Southern fraternity based on the character of Robert E. Lee hired a nice Jewish girl from the Southwest to tell its story. Because Lee was a gentleman, they were very nice to her.

Westheimer worked in a number of bookstores in Cincinnati, Ohio, her hometown, as well as in Colorado, and, being a better speller than mathematician, admits she has written and edited more magazine and newspaper articles than she has counted, including pieces for the *Columbia Journalism Review, USA Today,* and *Publishers Weekly.* She was a contributing editor to *America West Airlines Magazine* back when there was a magazine for what was then an airline (and is now American Airlines).

Her tenure in publishing includes co-founding BookZone, Inc., the Web's first place to buy books online (Amazon was an early customer), serving on the boards of both the national Publishers Marketing Association (now the Independent Book Publishers Association) and the national organization Writer's Voice Scottsdale committee, as well as Arizona Library Friends. Westheimer has edited and produced more than a dozen books.

Other adventures include driving to Alaska when she was seventeen (she had a note from her parents saying she hadn't run away), working as a carny on the Ohio state circuit ("Pitch till you win!"), carving candles for a living, setting type as a printer's devil, working as a maid on a steamboat (where she nearly effected a mutiny), and serving as "lovely assistant" to sculptor Kevin Caron.

Westheimer lives in Phoenix, Arizona, in the shadow of Camelback Mountain with her husband, Kevin Caron, a dog, and two cats.

ABOUT THE ILLUSTRATOR

Robert Chambers is an artist and illustrator based in Flagstaff, Arizona. He studied art and design at Yavapai College in Prescott, Arizona, and studied landscape architectural illustration under Mike Lin at Kansas State University. He worked as an in-house illustrator and in a freelance capacity in the field of ecology restoration on the lower Colorado River.

He produced concept designs and fully rendered illustrations under deadline for various state, commercial, and inter-governmental stakeholders, as well as illustrations for logos, tee shirts, public interpretive signs, posters, and other content associated with these restoration projects.

For the last ten years, Robert has been the in-house illustrator for Terra BIRDS, a Flagstaff-based outdoor education nonprofit where he produces landscape and garden concept illustrations, illustrations for K-12 curriculum, and other content that serves the non-profit's mission of habitat restoration and youth engagement.

He is also a freelance illustrator and educator.

Index

A

activities
  aerobic 71
  endurance 57, 71
ADH
  see alcohol dehydrogenase
Agasi, Suzanne 15
alcohol
  and bone density 58
  and risk of falling 78
  and sexual performance 76
  and urinary issues 51
  tolerance 26
  excessive consumption 51, 58, 76, 78
alcohol dehydrogenase 26
allergens 70
antidepressants 83
antioxidants 48
anxiety 96, 122
arc of life 84–85
arms *see also* bat wings
  flaps 38–39
  spots 40–41
  tattoos 42
  triceps 38
arthritis 75
artificial tears 62
atheist 118

attitude 8, 115
audiologist 64
auditory nerve 64
autonomic nervous system 122
awareness 8, 129

B

Baby Boomers 90
"Back Then" 104
bacteria 96
balance 40, 78
baldness
  female pattern 54
  male pattern 54
  and virility 99
bandages 34
baths
  as self care 49
  health benefits of 96
  ideal temperature 46
bat wings 38
beach 36
belching 74
belief systems 118
bending 56
bike 68
biking 57, 71
birthdays 95
bladder 50–51
blood
  circulation 47
  flow, improving 35, 77, 96

pressure 60, 62, 64, 122
  spots 40–41
  vessels 40, 50, 78
blotches
  from sun damage 40, 44
  moisturizing 46–47
  purpura 40–41
blue
  hair dye 55
  pill 77
  rinse 130
  skinned cartoon characters 43
bluntness 86
blurry
  tattoos 42
  vision 61
bone(s) *see also* fracture
  density 58
  healing 68
  loss 58
  tissue 68
botulinum toxin 49, 53
boxing 111
box jumps 57
breathe 63
Brown, James 83
buffets 72
Buy Nothing 15

C

caffeine 51
calcium 58

callus(es)
  and bone tissue 68
  removing 36
cancer
  breast 43
  marijuana and 100
cartilage 38, 74
cartoons 43, 122
cataracts 61
cell regulators 48
cells
  cartilage 38, 74
  growth of 7, 38, 48
  gut 72
  immune 35, 42
  loss of 38, 72
  melanocyte 55
  skin 35, 47, 48
Centers for Disease Control
  and Prevention 26
Chatty Cathy 88
chia seeds 62
clothing swap 15
cold
  compresses 44
  sensitivity 68
cold and flu treatment 96
collagen
  and calluses 36
  loss of 34
  microneedling 53
  moisturizers 47
  role of 34–35
  supplements 48, 54
  topical retinol for 47

computers
  and eye fatigue 62
  for note-taking 25
concerts 9, 21, 64, 68
connective tissue 38, 66
cool shoes 130
coughing 74
crepey skin 35
crypto 21
crystals 118
curmudgeonism 8, 104

D

dancing 71
deadly rays 47 *see also* sun
death 28, 68
decluttering 14
dementia
  concern about 23
  hearing loss and 64
dermal fillers 53
dessert 134
DHT *see* dihydrotestosterone
diabetes 78
diarrhea 117
diet 35, 70
  see also food, nutrition
Dietary Guidelines for
  Americans 26
digestion
  aided by laughter 122
  of alcohol 26
digestive tract 72

dihydrotestosterone 54
dirty jokes 122
discounts 91
divide and conquer 14, 110
dizziness 78
Doctor Ruth 125
Doogie Howser, M.D. 8
Doogies 8, 112
dopamine 83
drama
  king 88
  queen 88
drinking
  alcohol 26, 51, 58, 78
  water 72, 46, 116–117
dry
  climates 34
  eyes 60, 62
  skin 46

E

earlobes 38
ears 64
  see also hearing
earwax 64
eggs 116
ejaculating 124
elasticity
  skin 35, 38, 42, 47, 48. 50, 116
  and tattoos 42
elastin 34
elevator music 90
endorphins 83, 122
endurance activities 57, 71

energy
  cellular 70
  fast-twitch muscles 57
  from protein 72
epilepsy 100
erectile dysfunction 76–77
estrogen 98
euphoria 100
Evernote 25
exercise
  aerobic 57
  importance of 56–58, 67, 113
  sex as 124
  vocal 67
exercises
  arm 38
  balance 78
  box jumps 57
  hand and finger 67
  jump squats 57
  Kegel 51, 77
  kettle bell swings 57
  pelvic floor 51, 77
  vocal 67
expansive thinking 115
expectations
  abandoning 121
  birthday month 95
  freedom from 115
  societal 115
eyelids 44
eyes

bags under 44
conditions affecting 60–61, 62
  dry 60, 62
  protecting 62
eyesight 60–61, 62–63

F

face
  anti-aging treatments 49
  skincare products for 46, 48
  sun damage to 41, 44
facelift 49
faces, making 132
fair skin 34
faith 118
falls 68, 78, 124
fantasize 76
farting 74
fast lifting 57
fast-twitch muscles 57
fiber, dietary 72
fibers
  elastin 34
  muscle 56–57
finger
  callouses 36
  strength 67
flax 62
flexibility
  and vision 60, 62
  mental 128

floaters 60–61
flu 96
fluids, bodily 35, 44, 60, 61, 75
foam roller 113
follicles 55, 98
  see also hair
food
  fatty 72
  healthy 8, 62, 72, 116, 134
  overeating 70
  processed 35
  spicy 72
  see also diet, digestion
fractures 58, 68
freak flags 130
FreeCycle 15
freedom, sense of 102
free radicals 70
friends 8, 15, 18, 22, 24, 88, 95

G

ganja 100
genetics 35, 38, 52, 64, 70
  see also heredity
Gen X 90
gland, prostate 50, 125
glasses
  magnifying 49, 60
  reading 60
  sun- 47, 62
glaucoma 100
God 118

Greek yogurt 116
groaning 122
grocery cart 132
grocery store 90
gummies 100
gut 72
    see also digestion, digestive tract

H

hack, money-saving 7
hacking sounds 74
hair
    body hair, shaving 98–99
    coloring 55, 130
    facial hair, men 98-99
    facial hair, women 98-99
    gray "sparkles" 55, 110
    loss 54–55
hand
    callouses 36
    strength 67
    sun damage to skin 41
    writing by 26
health
    challenges 110–111
    heart 122, 124
    prostate 124
    and spirituality 118
healthy
    bones 58, 68, 113
    eyesight 62–63
    food 8, 62, 72, 116, 134

joints 75, 113, 124
hearing
    aids 64
    dementia connection 64
    loss 64
    and memory 18, 24
heart
    disease 78
    health 122, 124
    rate 71, 122
hemorrhoid cream 44
heredity 62
    see also genetics
higher power 118
hip fractures 58, 68, 78
hoarse voice 66
honesty 86
hormonal changes 54
hormone levels 38
hormones
    dopamine 83
    endorphins 83, 122
    estrogen 98
    serotonin 83
    testosterone 54, 76, 99
hot flashes 76
hydration 72, 116

I

illegality 100
immortality, feelings of 68–69
immune system 35, 42, 96,

122, 124
infections 70
inflammation 48, 100
inflammatory 60
infrared 48
injectables 49
    see also dermal fillers, botulinum toxin
inner ear 64, 78
insurance 91, 95
intuition 94

J

jars, opening 67
jaws 66
Jefferson Starship 64
jogging 71
joints 74, 75, 113, 124
jokes 122
jump squats 57

K

Kegel exercises 51, 77
kettle bell swings 57
kidneys 50, 117
knuckles 75
Kondo, Marie 14
Kroc, Ray 128

L

lady moustache shaver 99
Lao Tzu 121
larynx 66

laser facial treatments 48, 49
laughter 28, 88, 122, 123
league 113
leaping 56
lifting 56, 57, 113
liquor 26–27
liver
  enzymes 26
  spots 41
loss
  bone 58
  collagen 34, 116
  hair 54–55, 99
  hearing 64
  memory 23–25
  personal 28–29
  protein 116
  vision 62
  weight 113
lotion 46–47, 113
lung activity 71, 122

M

macrophages 42
magic fairy dust 130
magical thinking 115
magnifying glasses 49, 60
makeup 44, 47, 55, 126
manicures 36
marijuana 100
medical
  experts 33
  necessity 36
professionals 77
  treatment 62
medication 26, 40, 54, 76, 77, 78, 122
medicinal marijuana 110
medicine, advances in 104, 128
meditation 111
melanin 55
melanocyte 55
memories 14, 18, 23–25
memory 14, 23, 25, 52
menopause 76
microneedling 49, 53
mitochondria 70
moaning 122
moisture 47, 49
moisturize 36, 46
moisturizer 46–47, 49
moisturizing 36, 46–47
mood 76, 122
Mother Nature 36
moustache 99
movement 25, 78
movie star 41
movies 88, 102, 128
moving 35, 57, 71, 113, 124
mucus membranes 66
mummifying 68
muscle(s)
  and bladder control 51
  building 113
  and collagen 35
  of the eye 60
  of the face 38, 44
  fast-twitch 57
  fibers 56, 57
  and grip strength 67
  of the gut 72
  laughter, benefits of 122
  platysma (neck) 52
  and sex 124
  stretching 75
  strength training 113
  tone 48, 110
  triceps 39
  and the voice 66
music 64, 88, 90, 128

N

naps 24, 96
nature 118
nausea 117
neck
  bands 52
  firming 48
  lines 52
  muscles 52
  skin 52
  surgery 52, 126
  "turkey" 52
neckline(s) 52
nephrons 50
nerves
  auditory 64
  and balance 78
nervous system 122
neurons 24

neuropeptides 83
neurotransmitters 83
NFTs 21
nipping and tucking 126
nitrogen gas 75
noise 74
noses 38
numbness 68
nutrition 54
see also diet, food

O

OfferUp 15
omega-3 fatty acids 62
ophthalmologist 61
optometrist 61
organs, wear and tear on 68, 72
osteoporosis 58
overweight 39, 70, 76
oxygen 35, 96, 122

P

pain 28, 68–69, 99, 122
emotional 121
relief from 83, 100, 122, 124
Parton, Dolly 126
pedicures 36
pelvic floor exercises 51, 77
peptides 48
perspective 71, 84, 121
physical
health 71, 113, 118

"offramping" 70
pain 122
therapist 78
platysma 52
poetry 66
pollution 70
popping sounds 74–75
posterior vitreous detachment 61
pot 100
power move 134
pregnancy 76, 124
presbyopia 62
prolapse 50
prostate health 50, 124
protein
collagen 34–35, 36, 39, 47, 48, 116
eating enough 116
healthy sources of 35, 116
supplements 48, 116
public speaking 66
pupils 60
purple
feathers 118
hair 55, 130
spots 40
purpura 40
PVD
see posterior vitreous detachment

Q

quantum physics 115

R

radio frequency 48, 53
reading 49, 60, 62, 96, 102
religion 92, 118
remembering 8, 14, 18, 23–25, 52
retinas 61, 62
retinol 47
Retired Old Men Eating Out 22
RF see radio frequency
rhinestones 47
ripped jeans 22, 128
rock concert 9, 64
rolling 56
ROMEOS see Retired Old Men Eating Out
royalty 130
rubber
balls 67
gripper 67
scalpel 33

S

St. Vincent de Paul 14
saving 14, 90, 91
scale 56
scales 66
seeds 62, 100
seizures 100
self care 49

seniors 91
Senior Savings Day 90
sensitivity 68
serotonin 83
sex 51, 76–77, 113, 124
shaver 99
shaving 98–99
shoes 15, 78, 130
shoulds 92
silly 66, 132
singing 2, 18, 66
skin
   blotches 40, 44, 46
   crepey 35
   damage 34, 35, 40, 44
   elasticity 24, 35, 38, 47
   fair 34
   neck 52
   protecting 46, 47, 48
   sagging 7, 35
   tattoos 42
   thinning 34, 36, 40, 52, 98
   treatment 53
sleep 24, 76, 100, 102, 125
slowing down 70
slow-twitch muscle fibers 57
small and large stuff 84
smiling 83, 132
smoking 35, 42, 62, 71, 76, 100
snorting 74
socioeconomic status 102
sounds, high pitched 64

spa 36, 96
sparkles 55, 110
SPF 47
spine 68
spirituality 92, 118
spy 47
squats 57
stamina 29, 70
steamy 96
stiffness 66, 68, 72
street fight 40
strength 3, 70
strength training 38, 39, 67
stress 38, 54, 70, 83, 122
stretching 34, 38, 42, 56, 63, 75, 111, 113
stroke 78
stubble 99
subcutaneous 98
sun
   damage 41, 44, 60, 70
   exposure 34–35, 40, 41
Sun City 72
sunglasses 47, 62
sun hat 47
sunscreen 47, 49, 53
supple 24, 57, 113
supplements 48, 54
surgery
   breast cancer 43
   cataract 61
   eye 44, 61, 62
   plastic 44, 49, 52, 126

   presbyopia 62
swimming 71
symphony 74
synovial fluid 75

T

tattoos 41, 42–43
team 33, 113
tears 60, 62, 102
Teeny Tears 88
testosterone 54, 76, 99
throat muscles 66
thyroid 78
tiara 130
tinnitus 64
tissue(s)
   around eyes 44
   bladder 50
   body 26
   bone 68
   connective 38, 66
   degeneration 50, 66, 68
   kidney 50
   subcutaneous 98
tobacco 51, 58
toxin, botulinum 49, 53
toxins 70
triage 110–111
"triage the truth" 128
triceps 38–39
turkey neck 52
tweezers 99

U

ultrasound 48–49
understanding 21, 25, 64, 76, 126, 128
urethra 50

V

vagina 50, 76
vaping 100
video 57, 66
virile 99
vision 25, 78, 60–63
visualizing 24
vitamin deficiency 40
vitamins 47, 48, 58
vitreous gel 61
vocal cords 66
voice 66
vomiting 117

W

walking 36, 71, 78, 111, 113, 126
water 26, 46, 116–117
waterholic 117
watery 60
Waymo 132
wear and tear 55, 64, 68, 110
weight
    alcohol and 26
    loss and bladder 51
    and erectile dysfunction 76
    loss and loose skin 35, 52–53
    wrinkles, effect on 35
weight-bearing exercises 58, 113

weight training 111, 113
wigs 111, 126
Wilde, Oscar 131
Winnie-the-Pooh 42
"Wow" 17
wrinkles 35, 42, 47–49

X-Y-Z

yoga 74, 111, 113
yogurt 116

penstemonpress.com
info@penstemonpress.com

www.ingramcontent.com/pod-product-compliance
Lightning Source LLC
Chambersburg PA
CBHW080806120626
46556CB00009B/3239